After the Wedding Cake

The Couple's Book for Newlyweds and Those Preparing for Marriage

by

A. Ed Feldmanis, *MSW, LCSW*

Publisher: A. Ed Feldmanis
Copyright © 2016 A. Ed Feldmanis ALL RIGHTS RESERVED.

Book and Cover Design: Mickey Mankus
Illustrations: Michael Coon

The author of this book does not dispense medical advice or prescribe the use of any techniques as forms of treatment of physical or medical problems without the advice of a physician, either directly or indirectly. The intent of the author is only to offer information of a general nature to help you in your quest for the knowledge that can build a successful marriage. In the event that you use any of the information in this book for yourself, which is your constitutional right, the author and the publisher assume no responsibility for your actions.

Printed in United States of America
Library of Congress Cataloging-in-Publication Data
Feldmanis, A. Ed, 2016
After the wedding cake: the couple's book for newlyweds
   and those preparing for marriage
A. Ed Felmanis, 1st edition
Includes bibliographical references.

CreateSpace Independent Publishing Platform, North Charleston, SC

Library of Congress Control Number:
ISBN-13: 978-1475124538
ISBN-10: 1475124538

Dedication

This book is dedicated to my children, Felicia, Karen, and Rita, and especially my five grandchildren, Luke, Molly, Lilly, Josie, and Alex, for whom I hope this book will be of great use. I love all of you very much. I am grateful for my grandchildren and their loving parents.

This book is also dedicated to all of the couples who in various ways have shared their successes and especially those who have had the courage to reveal their failures. Thank you for your wisdom.

After the Wedding Cake

Contents

Preface

This book is an invitation. It is about marriage but this is not an academic text. This book is really about you. This book recognizes that when you and your partner come to understand ideas about what is right for you, your marriage will have a foundation for success. The two of you are invited to think and share what is important. So, first, you can count on me to tell you what I know and think. Then, second, I will ask you what you think.

The Changed Context of Marriage

For years good marriages and bad marriages just simply existed side-by-side. Almost no one got a divorce. It was a time when sociology-and I mean here the common sense of how we all lived and knew how our tightly knit communities were constructed-was very important. The web of family and friends in rural and small community America was fairly effective in supporting married life. This is no longer the case. The support for marriage from friends, neighbors, and family has changed dramatically. Today the psychology-what you and I know about relationships, what you say, and how you act-is really very important. Marriage is about what you know, how you speak, and how you behave.

While social connections are still important, they do not take the place of who you are and how you act with each other. I promise you that if you seriously take on participation in this book and work together using this book as guide, even with the mistakes that you might make as a couple, you can build the foundation for a loving, nurturing, and lasting marriage.

The secret of this book is that it organizes the most important challenges and questions and then guides you to unique, loving, and sustaining answers. Your happiness as a couple will always be based, I believe, on your willingness to participate together as a couple in solving your own issues.

This book came about with strange twists and turns. At one time, my work required me to call on people in clinics, shelters, drop-in centers, and various housing programs to consult with people in deep distress, to help them sort out their issues, make assessments, find them sustaining help, and on occasion hospitalize them.

During my weekly circuit of visits, I would invariably meet someone homeless following a divorce or married couples who had lost everything and were living in a shelter with their children. It was not, however, just the clients of these organizations who needed help, but it was also, as it turned out, the staff who had issues and wanted to talk. The many concerns included how to make their marriages and families work.

At one point I reflected on the questions that all of these people raised with me and wrote the approaches down and created a field manual. I carried it with me for easy reference and I could make a copy of pages if someone needed a reference sheet. On the sheet, if necessary, I could include a phone number where more help was available.

One day a very good friend asked me what gave me the most satisfaction and pride in my work. There were many things, but I included the story of my field manual. My friend challenged me, "Ed, you have some strong beliefs and principles. Take the manual and make it into a book that can help many other people!" So with this encouragement, the book slowly started coming into fruition.

What You Will Learn

Here is a list of what this book is about-the ideas, principles, and guidelines that make up this book. I also include what I believe is required of you to get the most out of this book.

1. Engagement-your engagement-is not just the time for planning the wedding; it is a time to create the foundation for a great marriage.

2. If you are already married, then the sooner you do the work in this book, the better your relationship can become.

3. If you have struggled through marriage, or have been divorced, you can make your next marriage better and more successful.

4. If you are a couple, not yet married, that is in a committed relationship, this book will help strengthen your relationship and increase your understanding of who you are and what you are doing.

5. What if you wrote your own book about your romance, your best friend, the love of your life, the one you have decided on? I'll give you some thoughts and starter questions and invite you to make your own album or scrapbook. Or call it your Couple's Book.

6. The success of your marriage does not necessarily depend on what experts say, but it does depend on what you say. Your voice is totally needed. This project, your labor of love I mentioned earlier, includes instructions, suggestions, and guidelines to help the two of you. Highlight and share the significance of your relationship. You can use a scrapbook, binder, an electronic recording, or whatever else you have that will let you keep your couple's book safely for reference.

7. To work, marriage must build trust. Creating an understanding of trust is hugely important. Trust requires you to speak your own truth even if you become vulnerable in the process. For both of you, your care and consciousness is necessary to feel safe in being who you are, without a dread of being attacked in your vulnerability.

8. All couples face frustration and bitter moments. This is a truth you must know. There may be, likely will be, a time when you look across the table and ask yourself, "How on earth did I marry you?" You may even think, as is sometimes the case, that this is the end of your marriage, but actually it may be a new beginning.

9. You will need mature judgment on your path. Judgment needs balance and a cool perspective. It is easy to say, "My problems are not as big as yours." Each of you has baggage, burdens, issues, and what is called a "shadow."

10. Marriage building includes community building. You and your children cannot thrive without help from and participation in community.

11. From a therapy point of view, most often the first person to cheat is the partner who is not doing his or her own personal work. Instead of making a clean and honest break, if that is actually necessary, or getting into therapy in a timely way, the cheating partner often finds another lover, often making the situation worse.

The most brilliant books on marriage have been written, so I asked myself the question: If couples and marriage information is so good, why are there people who are so unhappy? Why is the divorce rate so high? After thinking about this a long time, I concluded it is not because expert therapists are writing bad books.

Somehow marriage challenges never seem to work out right when therapists are right but everyday people are not involved in the truth about marriage. Obviously, if experts are telling YOU, the couple, what to think-even if they are right-then the big picture is not working.

Instead, I believe the best answers come from regular people being empowered with good information and struggling to create their own path. What I do in this book is to create a context, share my opinion, and then ask to express your opinion. What if I write this book and then, in a sense, ask you write your own book?

To Guide Your Path to Love

So join me, as you read this book, in answering some pretty big, important questions, like the following:

- Since more than half of all marriages end in divorce, what will make my relationship work, so that we don't end up in divorce?

- How do we make love grow, not fade over time?

- What can we do that is practical to keep our communication healthy and vibrant?

- How can we keep the trust and sense of safety that we now feel with each other?

The Seriousness of Relationship

A note to you couples-especially those who are a brand new couple. The question of how to nurture your intimate connection and make it grow is really very important. Love is the issue. You may have unusually high or unrealistic expectations for your relationship. You may even call it "unconditional love" but have little experience in asking for and giving forgiveness. It is easy to forget that neither of you are perfect and it is important to be able to say, "I made a mistake. I'm sorry. Please forgive me. I love you."

To those of you who are seeking a "do over"-in other words, trying to figure out life after a divorce or the death of your spouse-you may be seeking another chance at love. You too deserve happiness. Your learnings and your maturity can be a bonus in making your new relationship better. So, if you are also someone who realizes that truth telling-by that I mean speaking one's own truth-is very important and is something that many people are not used to, then, embracing your own truth and vulnerability can be an important foundation for your new relationship.

This book is designed to help you navigate through challenges to find the basic answers you need. Almost everyone understands engagement is about focusing on and creating a wonderful and successful wedding day and marriage ceremony. Actually there is a lot more to engagement. It is time for the new couple to build their relationship. It is a time to look at your life together.

I suggest it is your seriousness and your decision to be engaged, that gives you the right to go ahead. You have permission to start working and understanding each other not just as an "item"-that is to say, people who are only dating-but to start learning to work together as a couple. The payoff will be big in terms of solving problems and becoming more intimate. Even if working together now seems awkward, it will likely turn out OK and the good news is usually that it will get easier as you go.

Ed Feldmanis

The Sign of The Cross
The cross is a part of every culture and is found
in art of every kind. This is a symbol, a powerful
reminder, that great outcomes come from the decision to dare, to undertake the new.
It is also a symbol of hope and transformation.

In the work you undertake with this book,
may you find your love strengthened
on your path to intimacy.

Introduction

Author's Note

Symbols and icons, such as you find in this book, are
thematic and point to possibilities of great love. These
particular symbols come from my Latvian heritage and were
inspirational to me. Every culture, whether the reader is
aware or not, has similar kinds of symbols as part of a reader's
ancient heritage. These happen to be mine. Their use in the
book, are as guides and transformative blessings suited for
our reader and our times.

I invite your participation in the journey laid out in this book. This book is for serious couples. Therefore be warned: this book is not for everybody. It is, however, for couples that have made a serious commitment to each other-for you who are in love and want to build a future together. The book is designed to help you formulate and reflect on your highest hopes and best wishes for your journey as lovers and partners.

As you accept this invitation, you will be involved in an experience that will strengthen your love and increase your intimacy. You have no doubt heard the phrase, "Marriage takes work." In other words, you can't sit back and expect marriage to simply take care of itself. Profound as this statement sounds, many of you, especially younger couples, may ask "What on earth does this phrase really mean?"

The Work of Keeping Love

Almost everyone gets the idea that relationships take work. Usually people do not really know what the work is. This book is written to help guide you through the work that creates a successful marriage.

The secret behind this book is also the secret that underlies successful marriages: the better you are as a couple participating together in making decisions, the better you will build the foundation that creates both a happy, intimate love life and a strong family.

In part, this book is a marriage manual and in part it is a guided self-help workbook. I will share important relationship information in manageable contexts. Next, I will request your reflection and input. In other words, I will tell you what I know about a critical issue. Then you get your chance to say what you think about each issue.

Many times you will be in agreement with the book and you will be able to build on the ideas. In other cases, you will be able to springboard to a unique approach or direction for the two of you. Either way you get to have your say.

Think of it this way: I wrote this book to be a focused and, I hope, a vibrant, precious guide to your success. Now think about "having your say" as a creation of your own: a very personal couple's book.

Engagement is about taking the time you need to develop a lasting relationship. If you are a newlywed, your challenge also is to carve out "together time" to read, comprehend, and make decisions. You are encouraged to work as a couple, to read together and when possible to write together.

INTRODUCTION

You may also assign each other parts to do and then come together for reflection. If the working together becomes too demanding, I counsel you to have patience and to keep at it. In my opinion, marriage in our time depends much more on collaboration and partnership activities than it ever has before.

In most of today's marriages, couples actually share in doing all the work at one time or another. There are some marriages in which partners have specified roles, often spoken of in past times as "his or her jobs." In our time the conventional roles of marriage specified as his and her jobs have been turned upside down.

In part, the higher collaboration that marriages often require reflects the economic reality that it takes two paychecks for most families to make it. Neither one of you may be the stay-at-home partner. Because of work and family demands, your situation will take a lot of communication and collaboration.

Each marriage is unique. The big question is what will work for you. To develop your own unique understanding this book has "Starter Questions" at the ends of most chapters and important sections that are designed to help you get "your say." The materials and starter questions are presented and organized so that they can be used as material for your own personal couple's book.

The first chapters celebrate your love story and while important are also meant to be fun. The later chapters build on the earlier ones and involve more serious couple's work. This is where you two tackle real-life situations that you will face in your marriage.

Remember, as you answer the questions, you are also cooperating with each other, moving into the future together and experiencing bonding in way that allows you to be a more intimate couple.

Your reflections and answers to the starter questions will become more valuable over time. You can return to see what you each said, and it will give you clarity on your initial thoughts and decisions. You can then get a new perspective on how to handle a new challenging situation in your relationship.

This will be your memory book that the two of you will come to cherish. This album, your own couple's book, can take many forms but what it must do is have enough room to hold all of your information. Preserve this information in a place that is accessible and viewable for the two of you.

I have also experienced couples who have used their "couple's book" or parts of it to share their "own story." When you are a brand new couple, it is one way that friends and family begin to learn and accept who you are as a couple.

This approach has also been particularly helpful with various events leading up to the wedding. For example, I have personally witnessed it used very effectively at the pre-wedding or rehearsal dinner. As it sometimes happens, the people who come to weddings may not always know the couple well. Naturally these guests are curious and ask questions. How did you meet? Was it love at first sight? How long have you been going together? What do you think is so special about your relationship? Do you want to have children? How will you support yourselves? What are the two of you about?

The guests want to feel more connected to the couple to whom they are bringing coffee pots, toasters, and china. The wedding, after all, is an event for them as well. I have seen both family and guests deeply touched by the couple's sharing. As the couple received positive reactions from their guests, the couple has an opportunity to find an even deeper meaning in their work. They can create a bond and find lasting supporters for their marriage.

This Book Is Designed to Help You

This book starts with the basics of your relationship and then moves into the most important questions of marriage. Part One is designed to reflect the joy and excitement of your relationship. Here you are asked to capture and tell your love story. While most people see the fun in this activity, not all, at first, see that this telling also serves as the foundation for the work of later chapters. Chapter 1 explores the magic and the compatibility that makes you click as a couple. Chapter 2 focuses on your common experiences that have touched and influenced your lives. Chapter 3 helps you to shape your new identity and delves into what makes you unique as a couple. You will get a chance to review your romance and love and also how you made your decision to be a couple. In Chapter 4 you are invited to look at your own experience of couples that you know and observe how they seem to function and so learn what is useful for you.

Part Two is about the gut issues that give couples problems. These are the biggest and most common challenges and stumbling blocks of marriage. Chapter 5 is about the all-important topic of sex. Very likely you have decided to be a couple in large part because of sex. It is a good place to start because it is important that marital sex stay vibrant and alive. While this is not a sex manual, you will find here critical sex dos and don'ts as well as recommendations to help you make good decisions about your sex life. Chapter 6 deals directly with communication, and is replete with communication suggestions, hints and ideas. Chapter 7 is about money and how you can make decisions so that money is not the arena of warfare for you. Images and issues about money and money problems can shatter marriages. Chapter 8 focuses on the gifts and dilemmas of extended family and helps you come to agreement about how to handle the more challenging and hurtful family members.

In Part Three you will explore creating the foundations that support a successful marriage. You will get a chance to explore your own unique understandings of how you as a couple can create underpinnings for your loving and powerful relationship. The theme in this part is about the promises you make to one another and how it builds your marriage. Chapter 9 invites you to look at the most public of promises. Chapter 10 allows you to explore your own promises of love-the private, intimate and sexual ones. Through an introduction to the Family Constitution and ideas on deciding what you and your family are about, Chapter 11 turns your focus to how your family can function. Chapter 12 helps you grapple with how your family exists in community, how it serves itself, and how it serves others.

In Part Four, the focus is on giving leadership to your relationship. Life's surprises often present challenges that are big enough to have the power to wreck a marriage. Chapter 13 deals with health, love and spirit in marriage. Chapter 14 tackles anger, cheating and the impact of divorce. This chapter focuses not just on problems, but how to keep your marriage healthy. Chapter 15 identifies the leadership ideas and elements necessary to save and turn around a marriage that is in trouble. Chapter 16 deals with getting the benefits from the longevity of your relationship. Chapter 17 offers a vision of hope and reviews many of the more important ideas found in this book.

You are about to embark on the real work of engagement. For newlyweds, the sooner you read and use this book, the less you will be surprised and overtaken by unexpected events. Essentially the result of using this book will be an increase in the opportunities for you to grow in intimacy. Answering the questions in this book will create a road map for your relationship. Your thoughts and actions, recorded by you as you develop your couples book or album, serves to actually shape your positive future outcomes!

Loving Communication

There are so many ways to get a message across to your partner. Not all of them build intimacy. The connected couple shown here are sitting facing each other. In this action they express a sense of honor and adoration that they have for one another as best friends and lovers.

The pose itself is a communication in which the couple sits knee to knee, hand to hand, heart to heart and eye to eye. In this setting the most tender and appreciative words can be uttered and each can reveal their heart-felt emotions. This is a place where love is strengthened and problems are unraveled.

 The Sign of the Sun is a symbol of Hope.
The Sun is a universal symbol for the vitality of life
and the power of truth-revealing light.

May you let the sunshine into your relationship
as you record the significance of your love
and may it bless your path to intimacy.

Part 1

Your Powerful Love Story

Chapter 1

The Significance of Your Relationship

 I am the sunshine that illuminates and records
the significance of my love relationship.

Chapter *1*

*E*veryone lives life out of stories. Stories shape our growing up, profoundly influence our learning, our interests, hobbies, educational directions, career choices, and even how we find compatibility with our life partners. Your story and how you tell it can decide if you are profoundly happy with a successful marriage and a resilient family, or if you are miserable and see yourself to be in a failing relationship.

The secret in a successful relationship is that now two of you, not just one of you, are telling your powerful love story. Of course, how you "story" all of your situations is critical. And how the two of you tell your story is very important. Your participation and the stories themselves work as a foundation for your relationship.

Your Powerful Love Story Must Be Told

Do you see your encounter and experience with one another as a wonderful adventure? A celebration of life itself? If so, then tell the story! Your story includes how you met, how and when you discovered your compatibility, and what your adventures in dating were like. Put those stories into the couple's book you are creating.

Don't be surprised to find out that this activity has huge romantic potential. Putting together your story will lead to much more. Creating a couple's story is a way to successfully grasp difficult issues that eventually can make or break a marriage. The work of being in love is to find mutual ways to continue your love, day in and day out.

This book's intent, especially in Part One, is for you to identify your compatibility from which your love will grow. Many of you may find that some background ideas for creating your own couple's book would be helpful. The following may help.

After you decide to be engaged, it is not surprising that you have a laser-like focus on pulling off the big wedding day. The marriage ceremony is usually filled with hope, anticipation, and anxiety. Actually, the time of engagement is much more than that. It is the perfect time for discovering the things that are important to you as a couple.

When couples fall in love, often the feelings are so strong that it is easy to sweep both big and small problems away. Is this true for you? It's as if problems will magically melt away. The real way to deal with problems is to admit them, face them squarely, be strong in your individual and joint decisions to deal with issues, and collaborate together to achieve results. Nothing can do more to strengthen the foundations of your marriage than the "engagement" that occurs when the two of you decide to agree together that handling your situation is a gift rather than a problem.

With a divorce rate over fifty percent, it is very important for you to focus on mutual decisions of how you will share your lives together. This book is designed to do just that, in a user-friendly way. Don't hold back. Get involved-that is, engaged-in the ideas offered here. Even if only one of you records and writes your thoughts, it is important that both of you think and reflect about them together.

You and the Love of Your Life

"I am very lucky." This may be your very thought right now: I have found the right person to be in my life. You say about your lover, "You are a person with whom I can face the challenges of the future."

As the two of you mature, you will, hopefully, come to the realization that you are each other's soul mates. Soul mates know that keeping their love alive requires nurturing, respect, care, and work. Although many couples intend to do this, they later find themselves in divorce court. What goes wrong? And where does love go when love goes away?

The short answer is love gets lost in all of the mutual problems, personal baggage, and petty aggravations that all couples invariably face. The art of marriage is not simple, but the results of doing the work that marriage requires are joyful. The results can include decades of a good marriage, happiness, personal fulfillment, and better health.

Times have changed and so too have challenges to marriage. Practically gone is the small town life of yesteryear. Most of you reading this book today cannot imagine living in the one place most of your relatives called home. This was a place where almost every adult watched out for all the kids. In this setting a lot of people had knowledge of who you were and what you did. In America this was a place so small the lady who lived on the corner and Aunt Tillie and your mom-and anyone who had the presence of mind to pay attention-knew who you would grow up to marry. That was real.

In those times, the small-town social and economic environment was all-important. Marriage and family derived support from that social makeup. Most of us no longer live in the environment of small town or rural village America. What couples know, how they think, and then what they do, is critically important. Now, it is not the old social context that once so greatly influenced marriage, but instead a new kind of psychology that is of primary importance. Please don't make a mistake in thinking that family and friends, who see you and support you as a couple, are not important. They are. However, the framework that sustains marriage has shifted.

Look at what's happened. For one thing, whether we live in suburbs or in the city, usually the small town feel of life is gone. For another, we no longer find just living for survival to be enough. We want some share of the better life. It is called the revolution of higher expectations. We expected something better for ourselves and so most of us moved to new parts of the country to get what we wanted or needed. Today, however, many couples face the economic complexity of not knowing whether their child's life will be better than their life.

Most likely, both partners will continue to be employed in order to make ends meet. However, even in these times, with the creation of a strong marriage foundation, the economic strain and the distractions of the work place fortunately do not have to be so overwhelming that it sinks your marriage.

At whatever point in your relationship you are reading this book, you will find tools and ideas that will strengthen your marriage. PLEASE, do not be trapped by the misconception that your engagement is the time you decide only things about your wedding day. That is called wedding planning. This is not what this book means by engagement. Often the idea of dealing with your married future is lost in the hoopla of planning the wedding. Are you ready to reflect and have the kind of salient conversations that bring you closer together? Are you ready to create intimacy? If so, let's get started.

Your Preparation For This Work

Picture this book as being the place where you can access ideas-some of which may seem common sense and some of which may challenge you. In each of the following sections you will be introduced to a topic for important consideration. Each topic is in one way or another, important in establishing the foundation of a good marriage.

Following each section, you-the couple-will have an opportunity to tell, to write down your story, and to put in place your decisions or conclusions. When the two of you reflect, share, and write, you are literally co-creating major aspects of your future together. You already know about picture albums and how pictures can tell a story. Expand that idea into actually writing about your love, life, and agreements.

You will want to use the pages of your own album or binder to record your chief ideas. This could be your first family album. Perhaps it is the kind of album you get in a bookstore or office supply store. Regardless of what you decide to use, you and your lover will be making some of the most important decisions of your lives.

You know that marriages aren't simply successful on their own. They take work. I presume you wouldn't have bought this book if you were not serious about your future. Something very simplistic, especially when it comes to advice, would not increase your chances for a great marriage. Because you are really in love, you will want your album or workbook, your couple's book, to reflect your love and hopes for the future.

Here is your heads up! The following list gives you an idea about what you need to do, and what you will be asked to think about. Each of you needs to feel free to express yourselves. As partners in this process, you are encouraged to speak what is in your heart and mind. Practice speaking the truth.

What You Will Be Doing

Find an album that will be practical enough to be both a memory book and a future planning book. It can be a scrapbook, a binder with plastic insert pages, or any other kind of tome (your heavy-duty book) that can serve as a family book.

1. Plan to work together as much as possible. (After all, you can call developing your album a work date!)

2. Read the sections in this book. Talk things over. Compile your joint memory and write down the things you want to include in your album.

What You Will Be Thinking About

1. How you met

2. The magic of your love story

3. How you became a couple

4. How to observe and discover secrets that make marriage and love last

5. The role of your family story

6. What vows and promises mean to you

7. What your intentions and covenant regarding sex are about

8. How romance and marriage work together

9. Your personal and family sense of service and mission

10. What it takes to create a family constitution

11. Deciding what's important and helpful in couple's communication

12. What it takes to deal effectively with relatives and in-laws

13. Life- and love-sustaining money talk and money action

14. Sex and compatibility

15. Leadership, spirit, and faith in your marriage

16. Dealing with hard times

To further help you, not only will I share my views with you, I will also ask you to share your views. To help, I provide starter questions to make your thinking and writing easier. These questions will help you come up with the content for your own couple's book. These starter questions are designed to get you going in the creation of your own understanding and eventually to your own way of intimacy.

Invitation: Be Conscious in Communication

Finally, here is a tip for communication. Often you will find that using "I- statements" will help steer you away from conflict and help lead to good solutions. What may help you express your truth is the use of "I-statements" that focus on what you think and how you feel. "I-statements" have the effect of taking you, the speaker, out of the mode of being a mind-reader. They tend to keep you from projecting what your partner should think and feel. The sentence might start with "I feel" followed by a description of your real feeling, continued with "when," followed by a description of a situation, and concluded with "because," followed by a description of outcomes or consequences. For example, "I feel sad when looking at the color purple like this album cover, because purple has always reminded me of bad things in my childhood." This format can get out enough information without straying from the point.

Later, in the chapter on communication in Part Two of this book, this method will be related to both resolving problems and speaking your truth without being rude or blaming.

Chapter 2

The Magic of Your Unique Story

 I am the sunshine that illuminates and records
the significance of my love relationship.

Chapter 2

*Y*our special moments are unique. They deserve to be remembered and told. This chapter calls you to action. You are invited to recall, reminisce, and capture all your thinking by writing. This is the place where you record the story of who you are.

Breathe. Reflect. Take time to remember how the magic of your relationship happened with the two of you. The following questions will help you tell your story.

The Essential Story of Your Relationship
Starter Questions

These questions and all of the starter questions in this book are meant to help you create strong intimacy in a successful marriage.

1. Where did you meet?

2. What were you wearing when you met?

3. Who else was there?

4. Were you introduced or did you strike up a conversation at school or at a party or at a store?

5. Where did you go on dates?

6. How long have you dated?

7. What were some of the moments that told you that you were meant for each other?

8. How was your compatibility made evident?

9. When was it that you knew you had found a person with whom you could leap into the future?

10. What else was happening in your life?

11. Were you in school, or were you working?

12. Did your lover meet your parents? If so, what was the meeting like?

13. When and where did the marriage proposal come?

14. Had you talked about where you will live?

15. Where will you live?

This is a section where two versions of the story could (but do not necessarily have to appear) appear. Each of you might have complementary events to record, and each of you will have different understandings or unique memories of special moments. It might be easier for each of you to answer these questions, and then blend your answers together.

The Special Things About You

Remember, there are the funny times, the romantic times, and how loving, caring, and how happy they made you feel. Also remember the hard times in your relationship. Be honest with yourself and in your writing about what brought you through these tough times. The coming together of two people in love creates special moments and ideas. What were your special moments? How did you know that the two of you were right for each other? What did you say to each other when you decided to leap into the future together? Were there romantic times that are special to you? If in answering the earlier starter questions you did not express yourself on these topics, do so now.

Let the questions above start your thinking about the two of you as a couple. Use the questions in the paragraph above and the next two paragraphs to inspire your thinking and writing.

Music of Your Love and Life

It is not unusual that lovers' memorable moments are marked by music like a special song. Whenever that music plays it brings to mind how the two of you were together. Some people call it "our song." What is that music? What are the songs you share? What do they mean to you? Write down the words to the song. Are the words meaningful? Record them in your own couple's book.

Special Mementos

After a date, did you save theater tickets? Do you have the program? Do you have a menu from the most romantic restaurant to which you've been? Maybe you have photos of places and people that tell the story of your love. If you have any keepsakes that mark the time of your courtship, they are worth preserving and remembering. Put them in your book. Take the time to write a brief statement or two telling why the tickets or the picture are important. Mementos coupled with a story can sometimes even turn into powerful symbols.

Chapter 3

Deciding Your Family Identity

 I am the sunshine that illuminates and records
the significance of my love relationship.

Chapter 3

Capturing and Sharing Your Special Moments

*Y*ou have stories worth remembering about you as a couple! Not only are there all kinds of stories that may include your adventures, but there are also love letters you wrote to each other or love poems that are meaningful to you. These often are the benchmarks that tell you how your love has progressed and how your identity as a couple is forming.

What better place to put them than in the album that the two of you are creating? Stories, love letters, and poems mark how the two of you are romantic or creative together. Sometimes, however, it is not only the writing of your memories that has importance. It also can be the ways the two of you experience someone else's creative work.

Is there a novel you have read with relish? Is there an author that seems to speak to your being? Is there a piece of art, a movie, or a play that speaks to an important understanding of the life that the two of you share?

Your album is a good place not only to capture your own stories, but also a place to identify significant creative works that resonate with you. In many countries, families often treasure a poet, playwright, educator, or someone else that is a family hero. Usually this person plays an important and creative part in their lives. They may point to the picture on the wall and proudly say, "This is our family's poet."

Today, many families in our country don't assign such importance to anyone. Your important readings and your heroes do not have to be from any one walk of life. What they need to do is help you tell the story of what you believe and who you are. Make a place in your album for these.

Identify Your Unique Togetherness Starter Questions

1. What was your most romantic moment? Where were you?

2. Was there a special event or place where you found yourself growing closer together? What was it?

3. Do you have programs, ticket stubs, or photos of your special times together?

4. Is there a significant love poem that one of you has written, or one written by a poet, that speaks to your love?

5. Do you have a song, a love song, that is your own?

6. Is there a public figure like a writer, poet or someone else you both admire, someone you resonate with, someone who speaks to you and what you stand for?

7. Who are the heroes you admire? Heroes can reveal a lot about what you believe and what you yearn for.

8. How do your heroes help explain what kind of people you are, what it means to love, or what it means to be of service to one another and to other people in the world?

9. From shows you have seen, events you have attended, art you have experienced, are there ideas or words you can adopt to guide you as a couple or family?

10. Do you have a poet, a scientist, or playwright you will adopt?

Your History: Family, Relatives, and Background

In the United States, our citizens interact with people from every place in the world. It is often as easy to meet someone interesting from another country as it is to meet someone born and raised in your own city or town. Finding the right person and falling in love is not necessarily limited by geographic boundaries. Regardless of where your significant other originally called home, it is important to learn about and understand your lover's background.

Once people have fallen in love, there is usually a phase in which each partner wants to know as much as possible about the other. The lover's feeling might be expressed as, "I could use a lot more of you in my life!" Or one of you might say, "Tell me more about you and don't leave anything out!"

Of course, people are complex and the newness and excitement of love is often too heady to allow you to stay focused on your personal history details for too long. When your lover is from another country, there will be cultural differences. The same is true if your significant other is of another race. If your lover is from the States, it can often appear that the differences between the two of you are minimal. However, it is so easy to overlook those important parts of family backgrounds, religious traditions, attitudes and stories about money, what food is liked and disliked, just to mention a few things. All of these cultural differences impact your compatibility and future decisions.

In this section it is very helpful to describe each of your backgrounds. It allows each of you to get a larger picture of one another's lives and lets you "get a feel for" what you like and what you need to work through. It can be very helpful if each of you write your own section.

You and Your Family Relationships
Starter Questions

1. What is your background? Is your geographic origin, religious background, or race different from your partner's? Talk out and write out the differences.

2. What is it about your family that might be different in terms of their background and where they live? What do you find to be surprising?

3. Who are your relatives and how do they influence your life?

4. Where did you go to school and what was special about it?

5. What holidays do you celebrate and are there differences in how you celebrate? What is your family's religion?

6. What is your religion or belief?

7. Are there traditions from your family, clan, country of origin, or general background that are important to you?

8. What holidays, celebrations, and ceremonies have the two of you decided to share, participate in, or keep?

Creating a Symbol of Your Own

I now invite your creativity and daring. By now you have collected and created stories that are uniquely about you. You have shared your history and backgrounds. Please ask yourselves: How are you a special couple? How have you thought about yourselves in relation to others?

This chapter is about deciding how to symbolize your relationship. While you have been meeting together or dating, going to the movies, experiencing a concert, or eating at a restaurant, you have gotten a pretty good idea of what you are about. Now is the time to get creative. The question posed to you is, "How can you capture in an art form what you're about?"

I would like you to create a visual work of art that illustrates how special you are as a couple. The work of art is something that is a symbol of you as a couple and as a family. A symbol has at least two dimensions. It can be understood to be a sign. It also does much more. It tells a story and points to greater meaning. For example, think of the country's flag. When people see it, they think of the geographic place they call home. But it also recalls important stories of the country. We are not necessarily going for something as profound as the flag. What we're looking for is something that would point to you as a couple.

Maybe what other people have done will give you some inspiration. Many of the families that first settled in this country brought with them special objects that reminded them of who they were and where they came from. Some had an old family Bible in which family records were written or kept. For some a crest or other graphic representation symbolized their family or clan. Some have a special quilt or banner that was made to commemorate their family identity and marriage.

Even today some couples set aside precious objects that signify their love and their decision to be a couple. Sometimes couples make a new family crest or a new banner. It could be something they have framed and hung on a wall. This is your representation of your love, life, and family, and this idea is wide open in terms of creativity. Your effort could be very simple or more complex. It's up to you.

Two historic pictorial examples that other couples have used include the tree of life, and the lion and the lamb. Obviously the examples here could refer to something important to them and be a religious reference as well.

Some of these have been framed and mounted with the family name at the bottom or top. Let your creativity flow.

As you consider all of the objects in your relationship such as pieces of art, and books and mementos you encountered as you were dating, there may be some that grab you more deeply than others. Explore what it is about these items that may have a special meaning. A lot of the things you collect for your album are also important benchmarks of your relationship. They can function as signs that tell who you are and how your relationship is getting stronger. Then there may be some things that may function with symbolic power.

Decide to utilize the power of a symbol. If you take the risk of making a decision, finding the right thing will be easier. It is possible that what you choose will reflect or describe the very essence of your relationship. Whatever these special items are, whether they are already made or you make them, set them aside, save them, put them in a place of importance. When you put these together in some artistic way, they could very well work as your family symbol. Be sure to save it (them), perhaps as a picture or drawing in your album. Explain the love and significance these hold for you. Your relationship journey will inspire you to create something symbolic, so that when either of you look at it, you can automatically sense the importance and depth of your love. Of course, some couples find or create a powerful symbol for themselves very early on, while others develop one, as their relationship matures.

Chapter 4

Accessing Wisdom of Friends and Family

 I am the sunshine that illuminates and records
the significance of my love relationship.

Chapter 4

*Y*ou have probably met couples that you really admire. You may have seen married people who have shown a special regard for each other. What caught your attention? Did you witness a particularly caring deed? Did you overhear kind, consoling or compassionate words? Have you noticed how happily married people treat other people? Maybe there are several couples you have admired and you want to emulate them. If so, capture highlights of who these people are in your own couple's book. Your parents may be your role models for a good marriage. Or, you may not want to emulate your parents. Either way that's OK. Who are the couples that offer your marriage direction, hope and possibility?

The two of you may have different but important examples to share. It can be exciting to glimpse the possibilities of your own future through life examples of people you admire.

 ## Beginning a Practical Vision of Marriage Starter Questions

1. Do you know many successful couples? Who are they?

2. What features of their marriage do you appreciate?

3. When you notice them in public how do they behave with each other?

4. How do they treat others?

5. What glimpses of success or happiness have you noticed in couples you see less often?

6. Have you noticed successful couples working together? What is it they do?

7. If one of your chosen couples has had challenges, how did they handle them?

 The Sign of the Morning Star
This is a symbol to remember ... a guiding star.
When captured in memory it holds the promise
that no travail, challenge or issue is too great to deal
with. With this star you celebrate
the morning after...
after the great moments of loving, and after
the great victories of problem-solving.

May its promise guide you
through the biggest of relationship challenges.

Part 2

Choosing Future Pathways:
Sex, Communication, Money, and Relatives

This part of the book is important for those who are engaged or recently married. This part is also important for couples cohabiting and perhaps are all but formally married (ABFM). In this part of the book we look at sex, money, partner communications, and relationships with extended family. The following chapters are about the gutsiest, and often toughest topics in marriage.

If you are seriously dating, most of you will have begun a sexual relationship. If you have been together for an extended period of time you have inevitably talked about money. If you are in love and seriously care about each other, you will have had disagreements and fights, so you know communication is an issue. Many of you may already have met each others' families, for better or worse. For these reasons these topics appear now instead of later in the book.

A word is necessary to those of you who may not decide to formally marry. It is not important at this point why you are not formally marrying. You may call your being together an engagement; you may say that your partner is your significant other. You may even be living together and have already made an agreement about expenses, food, friendships, housework, and other things. I want to emphasize that this book is also for you. Perhaps you don't realize it. You are probably an ABFM couple: All But Formally Married. You probably see yourself in a serious relationship. So please take this section of the book seriously if you have hopes of continuing your great relationship.

There is a general consensus that marriage crises develop in four big arenas. The purpose of the following chapters is to give you early decision-making possibilities to avoid some of the most obvious traps in these arenas. Here is my conceit: I know both of you are pretty sharp. After all, you have the wisdom to read this book. Therefore, you know that marriage is much, much more than a fairy-tale ending. You know-the one that goes "They lived happily ever after."

You may have some moments, especially during your wedding, when both of you truly feel you are in the role of Prince and Princess. You do deserve to be happy. As you make decisions about how to resolve some of the thorniest problems you may face, I want to offer you some pointers to keep you focused on the possibilities of bliss rather than discord.

Here is a summary of what you need to remember now:

1. Falling in love has everything to do, first, with emotions and, second, with the clear-cut decision that you are, and will be in love with your partner. Love is also a decision.

2. Likewise, for both of you to be happy, it helps to realize that happiness is a decision that you can make now and everyday.

3. Marriage takes work and not just work on the relationship itself. Sooner or later you will be faced with the work you need to do on yourself.

4. You have an opportunity to learn how to use, if you are fortunate, your large, often overflowing, romantic energy and direct some of it toward building a sustainable, loving, kind, romantic, sexy, and intimate long-term relationship.

You may not fully realize now that there will be a time when the gal or guy sleeping next to you comes across as a frustration and a disappointment. Every married couple goes through these kinds of thoughts and feelings. Sometimes couples can forget that it is a great privilege to sleep together.

Chapter 5

Making Love, Knowing Sex

 I successfully negotiate marriage challenges
to build lasting intimacy.

Chapter 5

*Y*ou would probably think that we should be talking right away about how to do It. And of course there are basics to know. It is amazing how many couples are married for years but maintain a basic ignorance about how sex works.

For many of you, those of you who are really into each other, you probably already have some sexual practices going. You know what feels good. Some of you also may be realizing that sex is about connections on a lot of different levels. It involves your whole life, and how you are involved with each other and can determine whether you will have a lasting relationship or not.

Communication and Sex

If you are into it, you may be also talking about it. If you are not and are waiting to have sex, then this is the right time to talk about it. If you are not sexually active, then instead of speaking from personal experience, you can talk about what you hope sex will be for you.

When people do get married there are vows; it is a public covenant. Most people assume that takes care of everything. In reality it does not. The official covenant comes when you say your vows in front of a judge, minister, or other religious leader. The unofficial, private one is established between the two of you. It is based on an understanding, an ongoing conversation, and is about sex, intimacy, loyalty, trust.

Here are some basic questions that need discussion: How often do you like it? What do you like the most? Least? What can each of you reasonably expect? When is it okay to say no? What does fidelity and loyalty mean to you?

It is not just having sex that makes you happy. It's much more. It is important and only fair that each of you know where the other is coming from. The understanding of these topics and others like it, make up a broader understanding-in effect, a personal and of course, sexual covenant between the two of you. Everyone knows about the public vows or covenant, but what I am emphasizing here is that there is a private, personal covenant as well. In the next part of the book, Creating Your New Life Story in Four Covenants, we will revisit these and other covenants that build the solid foundation of success in marriage.

This is one reason why it's important to spend time talking and thinking about sex. Invariably when sex stops, it appears that for most couples the marriage is over. There are times when the sex stops because it is boring; it has lost its magic.

What's important? Well, a lot of things. But making the physical connection work and having orgasms are very important. Tragically some couples, although married and already sexual, spend years of marriage unsatisfied, and really don't ever understand. So rather than have your sex tank, in the long run it is better to talk and learn.

Sex Challenges

Here are two possible realities:

1. Both partners do not always achieve an orgasm and sometimes, but more rarely, one of the partners never has an orgasm.

2. The mythology about sex and the reality of sex are sometimes two different things. People have simply learned the wrong things.

Here is a guiding principle and, as it turns out, a very important understanding in having good sex: sex often fails in a marriage because women are both tired and not having fun. This is not to pick on women. Exhaustion can also be a man's reality. It is very important, however, to recognize how exhausting adult life is and how very exhausted women can become. Having a satisfied female partner is important. If she is satisfied, she will likely want to continue the good sex between the two of you and likely, you. her partner will also be happy.

As you may figure out, it is not always the case that women are the first to stop sex. Men also report various problems. However, if the female partner is not getting what she needs from sex, she may eventually come to view sex as work and tire of it. Infrequent sex is not uncommon in later years of marriage. Getting it right between the two of you now is important.

Why doesn't sex work? Sex is a popular topic and it is on everyone's mind, so what is going on? There are several answers. Believe it or not, we are all taught things about sex both historically and right now that are not true.

Wrong Ideas Can Sabotage Sex

Guess what? In the way sex is perceived and in the way we do it, it does not always work.

Intercourse in almost any position works pretty well for men but pretty much doesn't work for most women. This means that if the two of you are inexperienced, females will likely have a much less enjoyable time. The great fun in sex is usually the orgasm. The truth is most women cannot reach an orgasm through intercourse alone, though some small percentage do.

Here is the problem. Most everything in movies and literature that in any way explains sex has historically been wrong. People in entertainment have always believed that sex sells. Historically they, the media types, all had the problem of how to talk about it enticingly without upsetting religious puritans and avoiding censorship. So they decided to share the sizzle without the substance. They settled on a kind of formula. They created a sexual hierarchy. Here is the "Hollywood" hierarchy sex list that we all were once and often still are taught.

1. Intercourse is the real thing. A real women and a real men go right to intercourse if they want to go "all the way." Some novels even suggest that the rare and elusive simultaneous orgasm is possible this way.

2. Oral sex, the stimulation of male and female genitals by mouth, was for the most part portrayed by at least implication variously as deviant, dirty, sinful, strange, and not even real sex.

3. Touching, massaging, caressing, hugging, and kissing, if done in a limited way, was considered romantic and if done "heavily" was considered "foreplay"-the approach to the real thing called intercourse, the big so-called "it." Various stages of petting were referred to in baseball terms like getting on first, second, third base, and the home run was the intercourse "it."

Compared to life's realities, these sex ideas we now know are really confusing. Millions of people have attempted to live with this model. And no wonder sex for so many married couples did not work in the long run. When this model is followed, men eventually become frustrated because sex becomes more infrequent and women are too often simply too unsatisfied.

So if the old ideas promoted in movies and novels do not really work, what does? Well, what really works is actually doing things the opposite of the way the movie and media model used to tell us. Sex research has helped us out with this. Imagine flipping the "old-school hierarchy" list explained above so that it is upside down. Here is what the list resembling reality looks like:

1. Sweet words, endearments, expressions of kindness, normal hugs, and daily kisses are the foundation for sex and real intimacy. How frequently should you do this? Pretty much all the time! This first step also honors the idea that the brain is the most important sexual organ.

2. Touching, massaging, caressing, hugging, and kissing can all be wonderful and should be considered sexual acts. These are a priority without which almost all sex will eventually fail. This is such a big deal that the old word for it-"foreplay"-is inadequate to describe this reality. This is the real thing. Not the only thing. But the real thing. It is sex. Manual sex. This step recognizes that the so-called "hand-job" is not an afterthought or way to side-step sex. It is a hugely important first step. At this step both partners can and do achieve orgasm.

3. Oral sex is third on this list. Today it is often considered a kind of delicacy. While care needs to be taken here, this third step is also a level where both partners can achieve orgasm. This step can be hugely important for women.

Since oral sex can be understood to be more intimate and necessary, it is also a place to insert a word of caution. There are two terms. One is safe sex. The other is one letter different: safer sex. Safe sex does not totally or really exist. It is somewhat of an illusion, but safer sex is always important. What we know about people is that we all are sexual and we are all probably going to have sex.

Here are some safer sex considerations for oral sex. It is wise and much safer in oral sex, just as in any other kind of sex, to be with one partner. This reduces the possibility of sexually transmitted diseases and cancer. The more partners, the more risk. It is also a good idea not to have sex when one of you is sick. Most people who get what is called the HPV virus do get rid of it, and it does not lead to cancer for them. However, this is something that you can research to determine your own comfort.

Most women think oral sex is fabulous; for women it is called cunnilingus. Men generally enjoy it as well; for them it is called fellatio.

For women this step involves the direct stimulation of the clitoris. It is the area, the place, where a majority of women achieve orgasm. This is also the step where men can, and it is often wise to, allow their women partners to come first-that is, to experience an orgasm first. Since simultaneous orgasms hardly every exist, letting the woman come first is really smart. It is a huge step in assuring her the quality she may need in sex.

Under the "old-school model," the list I shared with you that doesn't work, men often achieved orgasm first. For men usually the orgasms were huge, and they had no choice but to rest for twenty or thirty minutes. Often the sex never got around to letting a woman have an orgasm. However, this is important: women usually love sex when they orgasm; they recover quickly, often more quickly than men, and almost unfailingly they have gratitude for this loving experience. Well, they usually ask, "What is it my man needs?" For example, if the man wants intercourse, why of course, the woman is usually very happy to oblige.

4. Intercourse, the lauded and formerly praised home run, the big "it," is still important but not as important as in the old model. It is the fourth step for good reasons. It is still a good deal. It is worth trying often and it is also a good experiment. Men and women can get real pleasure from this connection. If the two of you are fortunate to have an unusually good physical fit and both can usually achieve orgasm this way, you may want intercourse more than most couples.

The Goal: Removing Frustration

As a reminder to men, too often a man's complaint is that there is not enough sex and that so many problems and even excuses become more important than intimate times together. This complaint is related to the problems of the old model. Because much of this kind of intimacy is physical, without much sex, the relationship begins to drift. When women are really happy with sex, a lot of the problems with the frequency of sex just go away.

Getting sex right and having it frequently often helps couples shift into a more mature kind of love. After two to three years together, you will usually find that the intensity of your romance will wane. The spontaneity and lust in your sexual life can take a severe hit by your third year. Immature couples-hopefully not you-who have not nurtured each other and their sexuality often find that in the third year of their relationship sex really diminishes. You will likely appreciate even more the care and love of your romance in your first two years because you have created practices that will help your sex life in the third year and beyond.

The issue of being too tired is common for couples in later years. Often you may experience sheer physical exhaustion. If you both are working, the tasks of bringing bread to the table begins to induce weariness and even exhaustion. It gets compounded if you have kids. Getting past being tired is a huge sexual challenge.

Usually, you have not been trained to work smart and know how to rigorously carve out time for each other. Here is where patience and loving kindness come into play. If you do not give each other attention, and if you lose the all important first step-the "words, endearments, expressions of kindness, normal hugs, and daily kisses" that are the foundation for sex and real intimacy, your sex life can begin to disappear. The next step, primarily using the power of touch, also happens less frequently.

This may mean that you need to have regular dates and collaborate to do work together by, for example, sharing household work and whatever work may block out the more personal time. Set a deadline for spending time together. Then it is great to be able to lay work aside so that you, in the end, have more time to have sex. Sex is great fun even when you think you are not in the mood. Doing it and just starting it has a way of changing the mood. Can a scheduled sex date be as much fun as spontaneous sex? YES!

Making Your Relationship the Priority

Other interests can and often do grow to be too important. Both of you are unique and you have things that you like and prefer to do. It may seem strange to have this issue pointed out. But I have counseled with couples who simply do not figure this out. It is important to make the decision to change some of your time-consuming interests for the sake of being together. It may be important to stop at least some hobbies or extracurricular fun events-for example, bar-hopping and fun shopping or being really into sports-for the sake of making time to make out, to share love and intimacy.

There are things that can rob couples of their sex life. Making the decision to eat well, to avoid unhealthy situations, and to exercise, including regular sex, is very important for long-term intimacy.

Consider this: Many of you may be drinkers. If you have come out of a college culture or a family background that emphasized drinking, here is a heads up. Alcohol is a fooler. You may think that it loosens your inhibitions and gives you enjoyment. It certainly does, until that inevitable time when it doesn't. Alcohol should not be your priority. Your relationship should be your priority. Alcohol has a huge role in shutting down and destroying sex.

You may even, at one time or another, have had fun drinking and connected that with a boyfriend or girlfriend or a time when you had great sex. If so, you may think alcohol only relaxes you and makes connecting and having sex a positive experience.

Surprise! The more your drink, and the longer you drink, the less sexual capacity you have. Regardless of where you learned to drink--in high school, the college fraternity, or your favorite watering hole, and how great you think it is, it is an ILLUSION.

We ARE talking about sex here, and how important it is. No doubt some of you have gone through your youthful drinking scene and come out relatively unscarred. The greatest danger is that you may have learned to "drunk" rather than drink.

Here is what you need to know: It really doesn't matter what you think about handling booze or what you call your drinking. You can call yourself a moderate drinker or a social drinker, or you think of yourself as a regular light drinker, but drinking is what you do. The over-drinking always has a negative impact on your sexual capacity.

The names or rules or limits, however you talk about drinking, don't really matter. People do what they want to. Yet, if you are curious you may wonder where the line is. Here is a tip: if either of you are drinking more than you are having sex, you possibly have or will have a serious sexual problem. If you are drinking and having sex together, you may not immediately notice that your sexual capacity slowly diminishes as your drinking increases.

Alcohol itself does not care about what you call it or what your thought patterns about it may be. You may have thought "you had made a positive deal with alcohol." It is what it is, and alcohol does what it does. Alcohol attacks every organ of your body. I once heard a famous sex doctor, Domeena Renshaw, describe in a semi-joking fashion, "Every can of beer a man drinks hangs off the end of his penis."

Many people who engage in regular long-term drinking often find that in their forties, sex has lost its magic. Women find that it takes longer to orgasm, if they can do it at all. Men often find that their sexual responses are much slower and weaker. In short, alcohol eventually kills your drive and inhibits your sensitivity.

Nurture Your Sex and Each Other

Here is my list of positive things you can do as a couple to keep your love and sexual connection alive.

1. Make romance a priority.

2. Learn and practice the 15-second kiss rule: when either of you return home, make the smack you give each other sweet and long, worthy of a being in a Hollywood movie.

3. Give a true compliment to one another at least twice a day.

4. Say "thank you" often.

5. Say "I love you" three times a day.

6. Slip a romantic card in a bag or briefcase to be found by your lover later in the day.

7. Leave sweet, sexy voice messages that are suggestive, but not one too outrageous, and that also say "I love you."

8. Spend time hugging, cuddling, or simply holding hands. (Turn the TV or computer off.)

9. If you watch TV, don't sit apart. Use the time to hold each other's hand. Show physical affection.

10. Stay in the dating mode; actually make a date night event and use the ideas of courting and dating as an appropriate way to communicate.

11. Go on dates but do it alone without other couples. Dating is about romance, and double dating should be left to the teenagers.

12. Even when you live together and see each other everyday, send each other love notes and romantic cards.

13. Call each other often, daily; even make the quick call to work to say "I love you."

14. When you are apart, plan a reunion so that you might find some time together. Make the everyday homecoming a big deal.

15. From time to time buy each other a thoughtful gift or souvenir. It is the thoughtfulness that counts here.

Sex Is Not a Four-Letter Word!

Yet sex is the source of a great deal of social disagreement. I encourage you as a couple to do what is right for you. It is up to you to decide what you like and what you do, but I also encourage you to be as safe as possible.

So what is really good about sex for you? Have you started your sexual relationship, or will you after the wedding? Either way, when you start, I hope you will be telling each other what it is you like or you think you might like and need. Discuss and try out a lot of sexual ideas. Here are a few suggestions to start your thinking.

For example, don't be afraid to try out new places to have sex, as long as you are safe (and don't get arrested.) Acting out fantasies can be fun. My suggestion is to go slow and to talk to each other about what works and what you enjoy. Have fun with things like play acting and dressing up. However, know the difference between fantasy and reality. There is a time to stop, and there is lot to be said for whatever normal regular sex is for you.

Again, spontaneous lovemaking can be exciting fun. It is not the only way to approach sex, and it is not always the best way. Planning for sex and intimate times works too.

It is important that both of you know that you are healthy. Start your relationship by having a medical check-up. It's not really a big deal to do it but it is important to be safe.

It is fine, really OK, whatever the sexual background you come from, inexperienced or experienced. There are still things to learn. If you are inexperienced, however, don't feel left out, because the best is yet to come.

The Special Power of Touch

That special feeling of connecting, when you are discovering each other, is amazingly powerful. It can be a time when it feels like no one else in the world exists. One day I witnessed one such couple on a rapid train. He was wearing soldier's pants and she was wearing his hat and jacket. Her legs crossed over his lap and they were holding on to each other for dear life. She looked into his eyes and said, "You are my destiny."

More mature and sophisticated couples may see this and say it is puppy love, the silliness of youth, or maybe the first serious relationship. It is exactly couples like this couple, many of whom are "first timers" and millions of others like them, who at this point are experiencing a "golden age" or a "golden hour" of sex. It is a powerful, emotional time.

The couple on the train, like other new lovers, experiences an unbelievable connection. The young couple did not invent sex. Their feelings, like with many young couples, can be so overwhelming that they could easily believe they had. What makes these encounters a truly golden time of sex is that these young couples get so much right about sex, even if they don't understand or completely know what they are doing.

The secret and the power of your own sexual relationship can be found here. All of the best in sexuality, now and forever, depends on exactly what this couple was doing. They were obviously experiencing a lot, but especially the power of touch. From observing them on the train, for them, their embrace was like holding on for dear life and really, really loving it.

As you read this, there may be something in your own mind that clicks, "Oh yeah, I know that's true for me." Or maybe the last time you simply held hands, there was a rush of emotion that felt great. If so, you are connecting with what I am telling you. Touch is the one essential thing that new couples get right. It is also one most important things to remember for sex throughout married life.

Once the power of touch-usually understood to be the very reason sex is "golden"-is forgotten, sex is never the same. It is then sex just starts to become dull.

The Physical Goal of Sex

There is one all-important physical factor that is usually necessary in sex. It is orgasm. However, whether you have an orgasm on not, you may discover there are other paths to intimacy.

Some men and women have maintained good physical contact for years and have found joy and comfort in it and are very satisfied with their relationship. That is OK and each couple works out its own reality. It is my contention that usually both women and men need to have orgasms. Of course, it is understandable that sometimes some people, for reasons of weariness, anxiety, or other medical reasons, cannot orgasm. This is not the case for the majority of us.

The goal is to have good-great-sex! However, it is much better to have mind-blowing sex. It is not written in stone that a love relationship without sex cannot support a marriage. It can. However, most of us as sexual beings need sex in our relationship. It is not obvious to everyone, but a major part of keeping sex strong is that both partners have orgasms. It is helpful to discuss with your partner what their experiences of orgasm are, and when you first discovered yours. If you find that either of you are not sure you know the experience, I encourage you to be accepting rather than judgmental.

If either of you find yourselves in this situation, it can usually be remedied. You may remember a hit television series called *Desperate Housewives*. This show is now a part of TV history's most notable. During one hilarious episode, middle-aged Bree Van de Kamp, a redhead with a compulsion to always clean and organize, finds herself with a new very different, enthusiastic lover. After what appears to be a good time, Bree suddenly becomes overwhelmed and frightened. She rushes to the bathroom to check herself out, and the next day immediately goes to her doctor to explain her sexual encounter and states she believes she has had a stroke. To her surprise, and to the audiences' amusement, the doctor tells her she has not had a stroke; she has had an orgasm.

You are invited to consider it your job to physically nurture and care for each other. Nurture will help elicit healthy sexual responses. During sex, men can encourage their partners and even help them come first. Though men often pride themselves thinking they are robust and healthy, there will be times when women partners will need to encourage and support a man's sexuality.

Confusing Media Messages

The reason you need to know about this is that so many of us believe what we see and hear in the media. If you follow too closely, you will bring havoc to your relationship. You are probably conscious that media are teaching you about sex.

Newspapers, magazines, television, radio, movies, videos, the Internet-all have sex messages. Their interest is primarily in being entertaining and making money; so what is presented, whether implied or graphic, is often not reliable information.

Media sex is often just for show, for example, like TV shows done for drama or excitement and ratings. To know the difference between fiction and reality, you need to get and interpret what is going on.

There are ideas about sex that are something like a fad; they come and go. Take, for example, the myth that has been built around the young college- trained woman. One hyped story, a kind of composite picture drawn from various shows and magazines, is about her so-called increased need and demand for sex. She is pictured as sexually hungry and voracious. As the story goes, this woman is the new sexual athlete. Similar to what is said of the porn star, it is said this new woman wants sex almost all the time.

However, while some general things are true, the truth in real life is that sexual response is very individual and what's right for one person is not right for someone else. Another part of the story suggests that the new woman, being somewhat of an athlete, loves to be pounded hard during intercourse. This is almost like being physically slammed. While some women may enjoy this, many find it painful. The point is that learning about sex from media and entertainment stories is not the best option.

One of the most challenging themes of all is the one that pictures the new woman as a heavy drinker. She consumes a lot and it does not adversely faze her. Here the image of booze and sex are tied together. Surely the new woman wants to drink before and after sexual encounters. What is missing in this story is the idea of taking your time, getting to know one another, and creating friendship and then real intimacy.

Sexual women, those who really like sex, have been historically portrayed on the screen as harlots, shameful sinners, or whores. Of course, in real life this is not true. And sexual interest in women and men varies widely.

The movies have historically portrayed the idea that sex equals intercourse and intercourse equals sex. This, of course, is bunk. This media message might be right, or it could be very, very wrong. It depends on you, the couple.

The movies often portrayed bad sexual advice. For example, it was implied to women in the movies that "sex is your duty." In other words, the media message sometimes was "there is nothing in it for you."

At one time, popular thought, reinforced by the movies, implied that sex was only for reproduction. In other words couples should not ever have sex for fun.

Making It Work

What works? It is usually true that if sex does not work, your marriage is headed for divorce. Couples who have patience, take their time, and learn about each other are more successful. It is important to say that whatever turns the two of you on, as long as it is relatively safe and allows both of you to have an orgasm, is usually the right thing to do.

You may already know some things you like. We do know some things that don't work. To reinforce an earlier message, what does not work for a very large majority of women is intercourse by itself as a pathway to female orgasm. Only a small minority of women can experience orgasm through intercourse. Of course some women do climax through intercourse for various reasons. It's just that most women don't. If you as a loving partner do not get it that women need more than these old ideas suggest, sex will eventually become boring and a turnoff. No wonder married sex often fails and therefore marriages are often in trouble.

The death of marital sex usually leads to divorce. Why not keep sex alive and vibrant? Besides, it's fun.

An Alternative View

Keep sex fun. First, sex is a powerful way to keep your relationship vibrant. Second, it is often a motivational driver that can inspire you to resolve any differences between the two of you. Third, you not only benefit yourselves by having good sex, your children, if you have them, benefit by you being two loving parents.

Once we understand that sex is much more than intercourse, then we've arrived at a better way of thinking about it. Sex is about words and touch. This is a foundational understanding. Since the time we were new infants we thrived and grew only because someone touched, hugged or cuddled us. When babies do not get this touch they become ill. There is the failure to thrive. These babies can often die. All the way through childhood and adulthood, aside from sex and in just every day normal life, we have a real need for touch. That's one reason hugs are so popular.

Second, sex requires your active participation. Making sex work will mean a lot to you both. I suggest that you explore what is fun and what works for both of you. If one person is enthusiastic about sex and the other is not, there will be a strain on your relationship. Some of this strain can be the result of bad sexual information. If you or your partner have gotten a lot of bad sexual information it can take time to unlearn and have a change of mind.

We as a society took a long time to unlearn and change our minds. Perhaps you have heard this well-known story. It is now legendary. At one time doctors fully believed that orgasms for women were located in the vagina. They, at the same time, treated women with stress and exhaustion and called it female hysteria. They discovered that the relief for hysteria, as emotional weariness was called then, was to massage the clitoris. Sears and Roebuck made a nice income selling massagers along with its household items of toasters and irons. It eventually dawned on both doctors and women that the female orgasm is not usually triggered in or located in the vagina. That the clitoris is a woman's sexual pleasure point was a breakthrough realization that fundamentally, if very slowly, changed how we all view this history, and sex. Of course, for those interested, all of this information is available through the internet.

Sweet words, the stroking touches and the activity that most of us know as foreplay now is understood to be the most important activity. We now know that if we don't get enough of this kind of "foreplay" our sexual relationship will probably be strained and may eventually die. However, these words, hugs, caresses and strokes can lead to orgasm! This is "outer sex" or "manual sex".

Oral sex is now considered the second most important, useful activity. With it, of course, the intercourse that can follow can often be more exciting and powerful. Both of you can achieve an orgasm with oral sex. That is big news and very different from the old way of understanding sex.

Most women find oral sex, cunnilingus, can be delicious. In fact, if a woman has her orgasm first she usually will recover fast enough to stimulate, and bring her partner to an orgasm.

Some women report they have difficulty playing with and putting a penis into their mouths. This oral sex act is called fellatio. Usually after acclimation over time, women can enjoy this activity. However, there are many women who do not. In these cases both manual sex and intercourse can be good options.

Only having sex with your partner is the smartest approach. You get to learn and enjoy with someone you know and trust. While "safe" sex is an ideal, the goal certainly is to have "safer" sex. In terms of safety, manual sex ("foreplay") is considered the safest activity. Again, the warning about sex needs to be clear. The overall smartest and safest way to have sex is with your partner and not others. Doctors warn that having sex with others, even oral sex, can be a source of STDs. Among some people the idea persists that STDs cannot be transmitted through oral sex, but of course that is not true.

Keep it fun and exciting. Remember if you don't use it, you will lose it.

Acknowledging Problems and Getting Help

For some couples, sex is a hit-and-miss proposition. If sex is difficult, I recommend two things: a thorough physical exam by your doctor and, if needed, help from a sex therapist.

Some years ago when I did a clinical rotation in a hospital sexual dysfunctions clinic, there was never a time that the programs did not have a long waiting list. Sex therapy is more popular and more accepted than most people know. At the clinic, many more people wanted help than could be helped in a year's time. Sex therapy and sexual medicine have advanced enough so that most married couples do not have to be trapped in sexual dysfunction.

There are compelling reasons to know more about sex. If you have taken the time to research sexual diseases on the Internet, you have found some disturbing facts. Today, the impact on the world-that is, on every continent-of the combined sexually transmitted diseases (STDs) is as damaging as any historic major crisis including the Great Depression or a World War.

Historically, in the United States, we have been able to deal with most STDs. The first time in recent history people were really shaken by what we could not cure was with the wide spread infection of herpes. There is no known cure. Now, however, there is a devastating STD called HIV/AIDS. Again, there is no known cure, although we have medications to suppress it.

It is much safer to date exclusively, because while most people in this country are not infected with STDs, the number-one way to get one of these illnesses is to have sex with someone who has them. Doctors tell us that STDs can be spread by intercourse, anal sex, and oral sex-generally speaking, by the exchange of body fluids.

Sex Education

I recommend you take the responsibility to teach yourself about sex. On some occasions parents and even religious groups teach sex education. There are not many congregations insightful enough or courageous enough to teach sex ed. However, many are thankful for those wonderful, bright denominations and faiths that do. Nothing presented here is meant to undermine that good advice.

There are many fine books on sex education. Here are five of my favorite books and authors. First, there is Domeena Renshaw, a fine doctor and a humorous educator, who has pioneered sexual medicine and has run a sexual dysfunctions clinic at the Loyola University Chicago hospital. Her wonderful book, *Seven Weeks to Better Sex*, can still be found through the Internet. Second, there is a stupendously good book by two brilliant women, Marcia Douglass, Ph.D., and Lisa Douglass, Ph.D., sisters who want women to have the best possible sex. With their primary audience being women, the authors at the same time express love and care for men. Their book is called *Are We Having Fun Yet? The Intelligent Woman's Guide to Sex*. Third, one of my favorite authors is Anne Hooper, who has written too many books to recount here. One of my favorites written by her is called *Anne Hooper's Sexual Intimacy: How to Build a Lasting and Loving Relationship*. Fourth, there is the first wildly popular how-to sex book, *The Joy of Sex*, written by Alex Comfort. The book has been updated and is available on the Internet. Finally, my friend Laura Corn has written many great books, most of which recommend sexy to-do activities; they actually are great sex adventures for couples. One of her most well- known books is *The Great American Sex Diet*.

Addiction-Free, Violence-Free Sex

Actually, sex works well all by itself. Sex is not helped or aided by booze, drugs, or violence. The acts of sex are pretty powerful all by themselves. (Although sex could be helped by rock 'n' roll.) For the sake of keeping your life and your sex healthy and vibrant, couples need to see sex on its own terms and not as a part of addictions or violence. The idea that violence and sex go together may have been imposed by the movies of yesteryear, but today most people understand that acts of violence with sex are not appropriate.

The belief still seems to exist that drinking promotes good sexual feelings. It promotes the illusion, for example, that drinking makes a person sexier and less inhibited. It is common for long-time drinkers to claim they have great sexual prowess that they cannot actually maintain in performance of serious lovemaking. Failure to have an orgasm is a common problem.

If sex, good sex, is to continue throughout the years of your relationship, sex for most couples has to change to emphasize satisfaction for both partners. That is, manual sex-outer sex, foreplay-has to be considered the most important part of sex. That is because the brain engages in sexuality with the power of touch. Luckily, because men are usually so much into their partners, most men will do almost anything to make sure the woman is happy, including helping her have an orgasm first.

In the movie *When Sally Met Harry*, a famous scene portrays Sally faking an orgasm while at a restaurant table. The scene is funny but represents a sad truth. Some women get to be good at faking because the real thing doesn't really work for them. Sally, funny as her character was, may not be the poster girl for good sex.

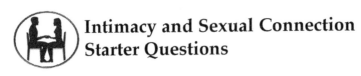

Intimacy and Sexual Connection Starter Questions

It is a pretty good assumption that the two of you have had a lot of discussion about sex. So the starter questions start at a higher level of thinking. As always, these are starter questions, so feel free to include and answer your own questions.

1. What do you know or what have you discovered about your own sexuality? For example, do you like your sexual self?

2. Have you experienced the connection of intimacy in any other context? What does intimacy mean to the two of you?

3. When you discussed your sexual partnership, what has been your agreement, your understanding, so far?

4. What is your thinking about being "exclusive"?

5. What do you, as a couple, understand your responsibility to be to enable sex and intimacy for each other?

6. How have you talked about a commitment to romance, sex, and intimacy? What do you understand about the two of you in this regard?

7. Have you discussed birth control, condoms, STDs, and the morning after pill?

8. Have you discussed the sexual positions you prefer and what you would like to try?

7. What are some of the many ways you have or want to enjoy making out, foreplay, and having manual sex?

8. Are both of you aware of your own orgasm and have you shared with your partner how you can get to an orgasm? How does it work for you?

9. Do you know whether you can reach an orgasm using manual sex (foreplay)? Have you tried?

10. Have you discussed fantasies? What would you like to try?

11. What's the difference between do-able fantasies and those that must simply remain dreams?

12. What are the important differences between fantasy and reality?

13. Do the two of you engage in verbal foreplay and sexuality? How do you use kindness, special touches, romantic gestures, and a playful spirit work out?

14. Were you sexually active with another partner before the two of you became serious?

15. Do you know what your STD and especially HIV/AIDS status is? What could you do to find out?

16. Has each of you had a physical exam and been educated about your sexual and reproductive organs from a qualified doctor?

17. Have the two of you, for fun or protection, used a condom? Do you know how?

18. What are some birth control methods you have considered? Have you decided on a birth control method?

Chapter 6

The Art of Partner Communication

 I successfully negotiate marriage challenges
to build lasting intimacy.

Chapter 6

*T*his is designed to lead you through some of the more obvious, as well as some of the thornier and more difficult, communication problems that you as a couple may encounter. Learning how to talk to each other now and making good communications a habit, will be advantageous in the future when your extraordinary connection with each other seems more of an everyday thing.

It is difficult to believe that there will be a time when you begin to take for granted what the two of you now consider amazing. These things taken for granted will also include a lot of acts that take communication. For example, even the privilege of sleeping in the same bed together can in later years be taken for granted. Can you imagine sleeping together can be ho-hum? Even making joint decisions can later seem mechanical and unexciting.

Communication firstly is about the *context* of love, concern, hope, and the intention of wanting the very best for your partner. Out of this framework of love, communication is secondly about *practice*, making the practice of positive communication a habit and making it your praxis (done so consistently, you could call it a "praxis").

Here are two guiding truths:

1. Communication has consequences and it is about impact. Complimentary words are usually helpful. Harsh words usually hurt. Words of criticism are usually the hardest to take. Perhaps the most damaging and abusive communication revolves around the role of the critic. Sometimes it is easy to fall into the role of being a critic. Most relationships cannot survive continual criticism. The perpetual critic usually kills relationships.

2. Communication is about admitting your mistakes. It is scary to find yourself in a vulnerable situation and have to admit that somehow you have made a mistake. Married life can be easier if both of you have a habit of stepping up and admitting your own mistakes. This approach usually works much better than shifting blame onto one another or needlessly going into angry tirades. Forgiveness in these situations is a really big deal.

Let's look more at criticism. Criticisms and the justifications of them can truly cause big rifts. This happens often when one or both of you continually play the role of the critic. Criticism involves language that makes one partner appear right and the other partner wrong. It is often where old anger that's been kept, stuffed down, emerges and is unfairly projected on your partner. It can be driven by fear and the need for security. The barrage of criticism, when it takes place over time, can so damage your relationship that it then cannot be easily repaired.

There is some way, even if it seems inconvenient, for both of you to stop your own flow of criticism. For the sake of your relationship and for sanity, you will need to undertake to do it. If one of you is the habitual critic, you will need to raise the question as to whether the relationship is workable. Deciding to marry someone and fix them later, is generally a big mistake.

It takes a special person to love and put up with a perpetual critic. There are people who can make this relationship work. For most, more than likely, a partnership with the habitual critic will be doomed without therapeutic help. Getting help early is important. The critic role is not one that can usually lead to intimacy or sustainability.

Let's talk a little more about changing your partner. This is a trap that some fall into. Closely tied to criticism is the illusion that you have the power to actually change your partner for the better.

The more you insist that your partner should change, the more frustrating your thoughts and communication will become. Although you and your lover are bound together in a journey of change, neither one of you has the power to change the other, according to your own designs. Your real power lies in changing yourself.

This story illustrates this point. I once had a client with whom I taught different communication protocols; I was able to explain how her husband was often motivated to change. I stressed to her that there is no way she could manipulate positive change in her partner.

My client started using forms of positive communication and witnessed powerful change in her husband. He became more loving and thoughtful. In therapy she had changed her husband's response by personally committing to the change in herself that she wanted to see in her husband. In this case it worked well. However, the lesson for many of us is hard to learn. My client still once wistfully asked, "But how do I get him to change all the time like this?"

Sometimes it is difficult to remember that you change yourself. You don't set out to play God and change your partner. For example, if you believe you must absolutely change the person you plan to marry, then your best option probably is not to get married in the first place. For couples with designs to live together, your best option may be not to move in together in the first place.

One more obvious trap is the belief that since you both love each other very much, you know what each other would say, do, or think. In this case each of you may forget to say what it is you need or want. This leads to a notion that your partner can "read your mind". While you as lovers may have experienced great sensitivity and great understanding with each other, no one can truly read another's mind. Each of you needs to learn to express what it is you need and want.

You will make mistakes in being with each other. The most positive approach to communication involves using words of kindness. Words like "I love you," "I'm sorry," "Honey, I'm running late," or when appropriate the famous "Please forgive me" are obvious words that make a difference. To be simply touched on the arm or shoulder can say volumes.

Actions also count. Doing something that benefits your lover can be received as a heartfelt expression of love. But even when your lover says, "Don't tell me, show me," he or she will also want to hear words that say you are still in love. Learn to say the words "I love you" and make it a habit.

There are ways to design space that lends itself to positive communications. My strong recommendation is that the two of you create a communication space or zone. Ideally it is a place where you can talk from the heart and not be disturbed or interrupted. For example, it may be your bedroom that has a couch or chairs. When you are first married and have the run of your apartment or house, it may seem unnecessary to set aside the den or pantry or bedroom as a place where you can talk. However, when there are children around or when you have guests, going off somewhere to the side will make a big difference.

When you decide on a space that's just for your conversations and your cooperative work, it can become a kind of headquarters for your joint efforts. Whether it is the bedroom or the kitchen table, it is a place where you can gather up materials, write birthday cards to friends, and perhaps pay your bills. Hopefully all of this can be a small adult space not meant for the kids.

Creating a Safe Container for Communication

A communication space for the two of you is a good place to iron out misunderstandings, to explain, to apologize, and to plan something different. You can make this a safe place, a safe container, where you can share your deepest thoughts and feelings. It is a place for listening and learning from one another. Here is the place for conscientious behavior. It is where you bring your best intentions and do your utmost not to attack, jump to conclusions, or make cruel judgments.

In cases where communication space is not available, at least try to keep the dynamic alive. You will have to make the space on the run, so to speak. You will need to keep and nurture a sense of your connection, privacy, communication, and decision-making.

It is important to note that neither of you are perfect. Communication can sometimes be blunt, but with time, forgiveness, and consideration, you as a couple can make it work. Making it a habit to check in with each other is also very helpful.

There will be the need for important conversations. You will always need to talk about how to handle a problematic friend, what you will spend, the planning of your date, or how to discipline the kids. None of these topics are appropriate for your children to hear. One thing is for sure. If you have children, you will learn that in spite of their inexperience and immaturity, the kids soon develop opinions about almost everything and they often want in on decisions.

Remember the priority is for you to talk things out for yourselves, so to speak, as couples need to do, in what might be called your partnership meeting. You will find yourselves needing to make some tough decisions. In the midst of these situations with decisions involving your children, one of the worst messages you can give your partner is that the kids are more important than your partner. A real problem can develop if you want to direct the kids to do something, and you put a priority on consulting the kids first, rather than checking in with your spouse.

When you do want the kids involved, you can call a family meeting. When you need to talk just to each other, and these occasions will be numerous, you need to remember to have your own meeting to the side-your partner meeting! And of course, all kids eventually discover they can catch their parents off guard, so that one gives the permission they could not get from the other. This is the classic divide-and-conquer move.

Kids can benefit greatly when decisions come from united parents. Again, parents need to defer to each other and talk things over. This gives you joint wisdom and often "two heads are better than one". In consulting each other you negate the impression that your relationship is about competition, and your kids can learn about cooperation from your positive example.

These kinds of decision-making meetings are important and usually there is a need for each partner to hear kindness and to be validated by the other. Even the least verbally communicative partner needs affirmation. An honest compliment or a thank you for a thankless task can change your spouse's day from negative to positive.

There are people who struggle with compliments, both in the giving and receiving of them. If you do not compliment or say thank you on a consistent basis, is it because you are unaware of the importance of this dynamic, or is there some other life issue that is blocking you? For each couple, there is a minimum of words conveying love, gratitude, and kindness that need to be said. For example, are you able to give at least two sincere compliments or expressions of gratitude every day?

Although many couples require different kinds of love expression-for example, touch or the completion of a task that expresses love-genuine compliments, thank yous, and other kind words are still necessary.

There comes a time in your relationship when you will need to say I'm sorry and mean it. This is especially important after an argument. I encourage you not to pretend that a problem never happened and ignore it. Say the words "I'm sorry" and mean them. There are times when no other expression will do except forthrightly and honestly admitting to a problem or behavior and explaining how things can improve. Unresolved communication problems can sink trust, create and feed resentment, and eventually lead to divorce. These problems occur when arguments go unsettled and/or stretch on for days.

Some Communication Traps

Arguments arise in different ways. Some couples have related to me that many arguments have started because of outside interference. These occur when outsiders, for example in-laws or people at work, offer bad advice. In fact, bad advice can sound convincing to one partner but turn out to be wrong-headed thinking. Even when topics are difficult, the best communication approach is to talk things out with your partner rather than simply acting as if relatives or co-workers are automatically right.

One of the big mistakes couples make in communication is in the use of projection. This happens when a person assumes or believes that using their own experience as a point of reference assures them that they understand the motives or intentions of their partner. Too often these assumptions are said as authoritarian, flat statements and come with judgments and conclusions.

In this frame of mind, false accusations are too often made. The fault of this projective thinking happens when what might be true in your experience turns out to be untrue for your partner. One way to avoid this problem is not to make flat-out or judgmental statements. It is especially important not to make them when you are angry because these statements can come out as belittling. There is a big danger in assuming that something is true, without having tested out the idea with one another.

In this kind of situation telling a person what is wrong with them often exposes what is also wrong with you, the teller. One way to save yourself from using projections is to talk things out, and listen to each other. The idea here is to ask real questions without being mean and playing "gotcha." This saves both of you from being in the role of "mind readers." Another thing you can do, especially if you can control your fear or anger, is to stop and reflect on your thought even if it is simply counting to ten or a hundred. In this way you buy yourself time for somber reflection. Please buy yourself time.

Here is what I am talking about. Have you ever been in a situation in which someone's expression generated a burst of surprising thoughts and images? Perhaps at that time you could have said something funny, smart-alecky, embarrassing, or maybe plain dumb. Perhaps, somehow you got a grip on yourself and decided that silence was golden and could be a very strategic move on your part.

If you have found yourself able to maintain this kind of control, you can save yourself from many disastrous communications in the future. Your reflection buys you the time you need to get your messages right.

In these kinds of situations with your partner, you may also find that you are able to change your thoughts from a statement into a question. This is helpful when a flat-out authoritarian or judgmental statement can really cast a bad light on you. In this way you can pose the assumption as a question rather then making it an angry or "I gotcha" statement. It is also smart in the first place not to craft the questions you ask anyone as an "I gotcha."

The best way to preserve communication and an open and loving heart is to learn to ask in a neutral tone rather than the flat-out saying of what is wrong. In doing this you may express real concern or you might expose your own ignorance. However, this is highly preferable to being perceived by your partner as being outright arrogant, or mean.

Serious communication problems occur as partners take each other for granted. Resentments can grow and fester. Soon the style of your communication can indicate large problems. There are some communication indicators that a marriage is having problems. One indicator is when the people at work treat you with more respect or kindness than your partner does at home. Another indicator is when one of you or both of you are kinder to your mother-in-law, cat, or dog than you are to each other. This may be a good time to weigh whether your marriage needs professional help. If at this point you are expressing disdain or contempt for your partner, please bring your negative communication to a pause. Your relationship needs help. It needs professional help now.

Damaging Communication Culture of Win-Lose

As a culture we too often focus on how one partner wins and another loses. We are fairly ignorant about "win-win" strategies in a truly shared partnership. One way to say this is that your marriage is not a football or volleyball game. It is not about a competition to see who is right. Couples' communication is and needs to be about cooperation.

Since elementary school we have been pushed to do better than our classmates. We are compared. Our grade is assigned for our work that denotes our value as students and as people. From this point on, someone always wins with an "A" and someone else loses with a lower grade.

Too often learning does not appear to have its own value. However, a dominant image is that getting the top grade does have value. Later, when we are taught sports, we are also taught a win-or-lose philosophy. When we watch the so-called big game, we root for our team to win and the other team to lose. We, that is, both men and women, are totally immersed in competition by the time we marry. It appears we bring the sense of competition into marriage, and family therapists say couples inevitably go through a conflict stage dominated by power struggles.

It is not surprising given our win-or-lose mentality. Believe it or not, in spite of the many romantic feelings you now have, most couples will engage in competing against each other, trying to control things, and/or attempting to fix one another. The point here is that all of these motives can lead to damaging communication.

Competition can be an ugly thing. There is also the temptation to raise the question of "Who is boss?" Truly, whether one or the other is boss, it doesn't much matter if the marriage disintegrates into divorce. Again, many couples do not realize that marriage is about cooperation, not competition. Currently, the old power struggle, conflict-prone, win-lose way of thinking continues to rock many couples. There is a solution. One good answer is that neither of you are dominant in your relationship but that you work out ways to cooperate together. With some insight you will begin to see that it is not important who makes the most money or who is boss.

Being lovers, partners, parents, and all around problem solvers is a big enough job for both of you. Never mind about who is "top dog" or who is the "boss." Cooperation is necessary regardless of which one of you makes the most money or pays the bills or fixes the plumbing. Good communication is needed for the sake of the family and its creativity and growth.

Communication and the Money Monster

Economics have always influenced and shaped families for better or worse. However, you do have the choice of not letting the so-called economic monster, the one that demands more and more, mess with your minds. In this vein, you may falsely believe that whoever happens to be the top earner is also the boss. Or that your partner is somehow "less than" if earnings are a problem. This thinking will only help deteriorate partnership.

The silliness and waste of time of the so-called power struggle stage of marriage is based on competition rather than cooperation. Money also plays into this struggle. Given our culture and our social learning, this struggle is often something couples must experience and learn from. If the needed learning does not take place, this struggle can defeat intimacy. It is a source of bad communication.

The "I-Statement" Communication Form

Here is a very practical tool that can help keep you out of many problems. It is about learning to speak your own truth. In this process dealing with anger and learning to communicate in helpful ways can be challenging. Earlier in the book, discussions covered the need to speak your own truth and to learn how to express your real feelings. The use of "I-statements" is a way to speak for yourselves and avoid the traps of projection.

Everyday practice of speaking honestly to each other can go a long way toward diffusing anger and resolving arguments. The "I-statement" approach can be very helpful. It is as follows:

1. The first part starts with "I felt _____.
(insert the actual emotion you are feeling-for example, I felt angry).

2. The second part describes the objective situation, for example, "When the door was slammed in my face."

3. The third part describes the predicament or consequences, for example, "Because I feel I am being discounted and ignored."

The statement when put together is, "I felt angry when the door was slammed in my face because I felt I was discounted and ignored." (Notice the word "you" is avoided when possible. "You" coupled with negative ideas is avoided, which usually makes the "I-statement" work better.)

In general, I don't recommend negative statements. Here is what a negative statement might sound like: "I get angry when you slam the damn door in my face because you make me crazy by belittling and discounting me."

The "I-statement" seems benign but it is actual a good and relatively non-offensive way to express anger. It works.

The "I-statement" used well can go a long way to keeping your disagreements civil. Often fights that are resolvable are made worse by the words chosen to talk about them. When projections, accusations, and judgments creep into an argument, the argument is often expanded beyond its original dimensions. At times, the angrier person might use the misspoken words of the other as an excuse not to resolve the argument. It might sound like, "I can't talk to a person who says such horrible things to me!"

The practice of using "I-statements," even when there is no crisis, helps us learn how to deal with situations and can actually avert many problems. When the heat of the moment has overwhelmed being rational, you are left with a communication crisis. Ignoring problems will not help. Usually, using sincere "I-statements" can help. Also making repairs with one another afterward is hugely important. Saying you are sorry in a timely manner is critical to regaining a feeling of mutual understanding.

Learning to accept your partner's contrite expression may be another issue. This is an issue when anger overcomes the ability to listen. Some partners prolong fights by not accepting a sincere apology. Sometimes they are way too angry. In this situation you or your partner may willfully not listen to the reasons that started the problem in the first place.

The Power of Reflective Listening

Sometimes it is not simply about having made a mistake but about being misunderstood. Sometimes the culprit with missed communication is confusion. It is not the intent of the message but instead the message itself that is misunderstood. It is possible for one partner to legitimately believe they have expressed something real and important, and the other partner heard something offensive. Even if you know each other very well, it is possible that communication comes from different points in your consciousness.

So to slow the conversation down and to get focused, it is helpful to say something like, "Honey, I want to be sure we are on the same page. What I think you told me is_____. Did I get that right?" This approach can help lessen confusion and allow for a productive conversation.

There are times, however, when the only remedy for this snafu of being misunderstood is a second conversation. The passing of a short time can bring on good reflection. Whatever was heard and then said in the first conversation that did not work or even made both of you angry now needs a revisit and repairs. Both of you need to be open to the second conversation rather than carrying on with anger that continues to block communication. This is a point where maturity is tested.

"I don't feel right about where we left things. Can we talk about this some more? I know what I want to say first is that my intentions were not bad but I said something that did not seem to fit." Or, "I think in our last conversation I may have started in the middle of the conversation by mistake, and not at the beginning."

Sometimes anger has boiled up and perhaps you don't recognize why or how this is the case. Anger can color a conversation, especially anger that is stuffed down. This would be a good time to employ reflective skills, take some space if you need it, and then communicate to make repairs with each other.

Remember, ideally, your mate is your best friend.

How Communications Matter Starter Questions

1. Are you able to feel safe enough to tell your most vulnerable or worst experiences to one another without being judged or attacked? What must you understand so you do not use your partner's vulnerability against them in a later argument?

2. Have you made a decision to speak your truth and do you practice, or rehearse, saying the way it is for you? What barrier within yourself must you deal with, in order to speak your truth?

3. Have you as a couple learned to fight fairly and have you followed the rule to make up and repair whenever it is necessary?

4. What are some things that repair disagreements? How hard is it to say, "I'm sorry"?

5. How have you experienced disagreements between the two of you? How did you resolve them?

6. Do you practice giving genuine compliments to each other? How can you remind yourself this is an important communication?

7. Do you express daily gratitude to one another for both large and small reasons?

8. Again questions about coming back and making repairs: After one of you has misspoken, do you know how to make repairs? What might it take to make repairs in a timely fashion?

9. Do you see the importance of not taking each other for granted? How would you find some time to talk and connect, rather than spending all of your time working and being too busy for each other?

10. Have you identified people that you think communicate well? Who are they and what do they do as good communicators?

11. From the above communication guidelines, which do you identify as important for you? Which are the least important?

12. If you find it difficult to give compliments, how about brainstorming a list of things that you would offer up as compliments? What are positive things your partner says or does that you appreciate?

13. Do you come from a family that says "thank you" on a daily basis and/or is this concept difficult for you? If difficult, what might you do or say to make it easier?

14. Have you had time to discuss important issues with each other? Do you want children? Where will you live? What are your biggest dreams?

15. Have you experienced real failures in communication? What were they? Can you make a list of your own communication traps to avoid?

Chapter 7

Couples, Money, and Marriage

 I successfully negotiate marriage challenges
to build lasting intimacy.

Chapter 7

*M*any of you may have already had beginning conversations about money. Some of you may be living together and are figuring out how to split money and bills. Often money is easy to figure out. However, when there is conflict about money, money becomes a hot topic. That is the reason that this chapter shows up earlier rather than later in this book.

Special note one: If you are someone who has a plan for your money, whether someone else likes it, does not like it, or is indifferent about it, it is your plan. Having a plan is probably better than not having a plan.

Special note two: The purpose of bringing money into the marriage discussion is to help you clarify values and set your own realistic priorities. If you are or will be working with a financial professional and you find he or she will not help you figure out your values and priorities and still wants to sell you something, my advice is to run. Run away from that person. You do not need that person's bias and certainly not any misinformation.

If you are new at relationships, it may come as a surprise to you how big and contentious money issues are. You may put your whole relationship in jeopardy if you don't have money conversations now and don't come to basic agreements about money.

Perhaps you have discussed money issues and this might not be completely new to you. Consider that millions will start married life without any serious discussion about finances. So here are the reasons why the topic of money is important to you and your marriage:

1. Money disagreements play a big role in arguments and divorce.

2. It surprises many couples that they actually disagree about choices, preferences, and values. What money is spent on is the source of arguments. The two of you very likely have different values and this is not uncommon.

3. There are money traps that couples, especially those who struggle with making ends meet, could avoid.

4. There are simple saving strategies that couples need to know about that are vital for assuring a healthier marriage.

5. Your personal story about money and the roles you play as marriage partners are important to understand. You may think you are aware of your thoughts about who pays for what and who earns what. However, the new economic reality has overturned our sense about money roles.

6. The role that communications plays is critical and important. The more you agree, and are, in effect, on the same page concerning money, the more likely you will create financial security. Usually couples who consistently argue will also likely not achieve financial stability.

Of course, there will always be couples that do not follow these ideas but still have pretty good marriages. They may be lucky or simply exceptions. However, since money issues blow up so many relationships I encourage you to discuss money and finances early in your engagement or as early as possible in your marriage.

If you are in effect an ABFM couple (that is, you have been together a significant time and you are ABFM--all but formally married), it is good to discuss your money relationship as fully as possible.

Here are some givens that you may already know:

One or both of you need a job and to have income to cover the basics of food, clothing, shelter, transportation, utilities, and insurance. All of us could use more money. The challenge most often is to learn that the money you earn has to be adequate (even if it is only for now) and you can make it on what you have. By the way, there are even millionaires who think they do not have enough and cannot make ends meet. Learning to be money smart is the key. You need to make a budget and know that it is a road map and not a "law."

Your spending priorities at first may seem impossible to decide upon and you may feel that the two of you are in conflict over what is important. Making a budget regularly can teach lessons about what works and does not work. A budget can be a great learning tool. There is never a perfect budget. Budgets are all about the learning. Have conversations about money and values. This is where you gain wisdom, build trust, and create a larger sense of intimacy. You will, if you are to keep your love life alive, learn to compromise. You will learn that your personal values, druthers, and wishes are not always the best choices.

The ideas about how you work together and how you use money are subject to trial and error. Of all of the big conversations you have, including ones about sex or about relatives, the times you spend talking about money can be the hardest, especially at first. You may find that you now need the communication ideas found in earlier chapters of this book.

Money Strategies for New Couples

Here are strategies that boost stability of your marriage. And as always, if these do not work for you, create your own.

1. Talk it over.

Simple? I encourage you to discuss all the issues you have about money. There are times when it is especially important. For example, couples often wind up fighting when one or both of you lose a job. When you feel desperate, it is easy to blame instead of trying to understand. Suddenly during economic recessions and depressions millions of us are shocked to find ourselves out of work.

Another reason to talk is so that you can make better choices. When you were single, you did not have to check in with anyone about what you spent money on. Now that you are married, you are not free to do just anything you want. If you have joint goals and want, for example, to start a family, you will need to start understanding each others' choices and preferences. This section is all about not letting money issues destroy your marriage.

2. Choose the right bank or credit union.

You need to decide the basics. A really good question is: Will each of you begin your marriage with your own account and eventually have a joint account, or will the two of you have joint savings and checking accounts?

For the millions of you who will struggle to pay all your bills, having one checking and savings account between you, could be the smarter way to go. Consider as a general rule: the more accounts you have, the more you are charged in fees and the more you have to pay attention to those accounts.

Along with getting the family bank accounts is choosing the right bank or credit union. This is not necessarily one of the first things you need to decide but one that is important. You need to know whether you like the people who work at your credit union or bank. Liking people is a general indicator for whether you can talk to these people when you need to, and whether you trust them. It is usually not worth banking with people you don't like.

In choosing a place to put your money, consider smaller local community banks or even a company or area credit union. There is usually a notably lower fee structure, and if you are a part of a credit union, many services are free. The credit union is an actual co-op of which you are both a customer and owner.

3. Pay yourself first.

Many married couples remember growing up in a family that struggled with bills every week and every month. Before you create the bills to pay, like during your engagement, or early in your marriage before you have made too many decisions and created too many problems, you can create savings goals. This is a great opportunity if you are engaged because starting early puts you ahead of the game.

Choosing, for example, ten percent of your income, as a savings goal is not as hard as it seems. The way you could work it is to get your bank or credit union to help. They could take the checks you deposit and transfer whatever amount you have decided into your savings account. They can even help you with Certificates of Deposit. Letting them do it makes it easy and it is very effective. (Remember at this level we are talking about your stability and financial savings. It is not about investing for big returns.)

4. Create your money goals.

How important is it to have an emergency fund, to save for the deductibles for your insurance policy, and to begin a down payment account to buy your house? Not thinking about these things early and not making a payment to savings first, is where many couples lose in their financial planning. Too many lose at the very beginning of their relationship. If you come from a poor state or from a situation of poverty, not figuring out your money goals early can be a problem.

Decide on your targets at the beginning, saving for one priority at a time. Then you can figure out what you have left to live on. You should not be broke, but if you want to achieve your goals, living within your means is okay.

5. Bring in two incomes but live on one salary.

Naturally, this is an exciting possibility, but may not work for everyone. This strategy could be important for couples who do not have parents to help out in the beginning.

This is a tough trick if you have to scrimp to get by. However, it is how many couples have established an emergency fund and gotten enough money together to buy a home. For example, in the case of getting a home, the more you save and the bigger your down payment, the cheaper your monthly payment will be.

Fortunately, as the economy mends, unemployment will drop. In the future, it is likely that saving a full one year of your expenses will be adequate for an emergency fund. However, usually any amount in an emergency fund is better than no fund at all. BTW, the old recommended standard to save at one time was for six months' worth of expenses but in today's climate saving for a longer period makes sense.

If buying a house is for you, the "window-shopping approach" can help. You can choose a house that appeals to you and figure out what a down payment would be. This would create a reasonable savings goal.

6. Share living space to save on expenses.

You might think, for example, that it is a horrible idea to live with your parents. But ... if this idea is at all palatable, then two of you living, say, in your parent's basement is actually a great idea. Your contribution to food and rent is likely going to be less than anywhere else and a stay of one to three years, for example, can really boost you to saving a crucial amount to get to your goals. Combining your two incomes and shared living space approach can be very powerful.

7. Pay for big-ticket items.

This is a strategy that flies in the face of some so-called common wisdom and certainly most advertising. Many people encourage you to create credit to buy an appliance or even start your own credit card. There are shameful, aggressive promotions while you are younger (and even while you are in college) to hook you on your own credit card. Remember the saying, "If it looks too good to be true, it probably is."

Have you noticed the flier miles offered by credit card companies? Most people who pay off their debt each month can benefit from these. Millions of young married couples who are caught in credit card debt will struggle and often miss paying their credit card bills on time. They will, therefore, pay more interest and possibly penalty fees. You may even be allotted a higher interest payment. You may be the ones who are buying the airline trips and vacations for folks who are better off!

Here are two approaches to getting ahead on big ticket items. One is to **pay cash** and the other, when it is necessary to **buy down** the debt amount. When you use credit you see the beautiful washing machine but what you don't see is the debt load. You are actually buying the debt load; to repeat, you are buying debt load and not simply the washer. Credit cards sell debt. The very worst situation is to think of a credit card as an emergency fall back and not actually have a monthly savings plan.

Your first item and possibly big temptation may be to put your wedding expenses on credit. If at all possible, I encourage you to save and actually pay for your wedding. If it is paid for by your parents, do not look a gift horse in the mouth. Say thank you. However, if your parents are going to charge it, please have some compassion. If they are well off, that's OK. However, it is just as bad for elders to be trapped in heavy credit debt as it is for a couple starting out.

What items can actually be paid for? Well the list is interesting. And deciding not buy on credit and not to potentially keep paying for your goods many times over means paying cash. This could include items like your washer, dryer, and dishwasher. It could even include your car.

The car and cash strategy is one of the toughest strategies to explain. Consider that many parents of well-to-do families gift their children with washers, dryers, and all sorts of other things. They even give their children down payments for things like cars or their first house.

But for other couples the credit temptation can be great. After all, you have to start your household. Your two jobs may be entry-level and so you are scrambling to find money. Credit looks very good. Why not buy the TV with 90 days interest-free and payments thereafter to pay until kingdom come? Except, the problem for you as a young couple is that your personal cost of living begins to skyrocket. You need to make judicious decisions on whether you will use credit.

There is a great tradition of buying a car with credit. Now what I am going to tell you probably sounds counterintuitive. A lot of experts, looking at the financial picture over a period of many years, encourage you to buy your car and use cash. It is very hard to believe that it is best not to use credit, although it is financially smart as so many experts tell us, and to pay for a car with cash. In most cases, people are interested in getting a new car and are tired of the old one. However, continuing to pay off new car debt can be more expensive than fixing the car you have. These days car motors can last well over 200,000 miles. In a changing economy with deep finance discounts, it may not always be true that fixing a car is cheaper than paying off the debt on a new car loan, but it generally is.

If you really want to have big money to your name and be able to retire with some comfort, according to some financial gurus, the idea is to buy a car you can afford and then when ready, trade it off or up and buy a somewhat better car that you can afford and so on.

Many couples who have decided to be in debt and already start off being squeezed, may say they have no other choice. "We are caught so we have to buy on credit," they explain. "After all, doesn't everybody buy cars on credit?" It is a tough situation and many couples years later, pay off their debts and start to become financially more comfortable.

For those of you who live in big cities with public transportation such as rapid trains and buses, you can save a huge amount of money annually by taking public transit. It is often cheaper to park the car instead of pay for gas, parking, and other expenses.

What makes this buy-with-cash strategy tougher to appreciate is that couples who do not have savings goals and do not follow a regular savings plan do not see the evidence that they are winning when they buy with cash. However, some financial experts suggest that having a savings plan and paying cash for things (especially the car) can over decades, by itself, pay for your entire retirement. One reason people do not appreciate the big savings that can take place is that they do not appreciate how compound interest and other time factors of money work to their benefit.

Because you have cash, you can often negotiate lower prices on all kinds of items. Think about this. Does a store really want to see you put your cash in your pocket and walk out? (Generally speaking, the two areas in which to borrow money are buying a home and, if necessary, paying for a college education.) If you cannot save money by buying things with cash and merchants will not sell to you without a card, then don't use a credit card. Instead use a card that represents your checking account, so you are not using credit.

There is one more approach on the "pay for it strategy." Say there is a time when you are stretched to the limit but have some money put aside. And say your washing machine is broken and you know it is not worth fixing. You may be financially up against a wall. A last resort but the best one available is to use savings for an unusually large down payment. If you absolutely have to finance, it is better to put a lot of money down. The monthly payments on the rest will be much lower. If you have to absolutely finance, check out your credit union to see if the rest of the money you need is cheaper there. In any case this often beats simply using a credit card.

8. Buy used or second-hand.

This strategy can involve shame for some people and it defeats the idea that we are "keeping up with the Jones." For example, buying your first washer and dryer can be quite expensive. If you buy a second-hand re-worked machine, it is possible to buy at half the price or less; if you are lucky, you still have a very satisfactory operating life. There are small business entrepreneurs who actually rebuild washers and dryers. Often they offer good buys.

Buying older cars can also be financially smart. The difference in price between a new car and a one-year-old car is pretty substantial. If you are starting out, buying furniture can be pricey. Second-hand furniture can be a good option. Stores like those the Salvation Army runs may be your ticket. Also there are dealers who sell furniture that formerly came from hotels. These can be very good buys.

Here is another possibility at which some cringe but is a very effective idea. Most cities have shops that sell second-hand but good clothes. This again is a very smart financial strategy. It has also been a huge benefit, for example, to couples starting out on minimum wage.

9. Create your own "couple's container" safe enough to plan together.

The idea of a container is that it is both the place where you communicate and work together and the dynamic that allows you to understand that you can really talk to each other. This could be a weekly or bi-weekly meeting, for example.

Bringing up this idea as a strategy may seem strange to you. I encourage you to look around at what happens to couples and people in general. One of the major reasons anyone is fighting almost anywhere is about money. Whether it is the people in the local church, the civic club, or any other organization, the most likely topic of fighting will be money choices.

While this idea of a safe place to talk and work is covered in the chapter on communication, it is vitally important in money. The basic agreement that I encourage you to make is to reserve judgment and agree not to make your partner feel uncomfortable and especially belittled. Here is the truth: both of you will come to a place at some time where you are vulnerable. Being accepting of each other is important.

10. Talk about money and take practical action.

What do you do and what do you talk about? You talk about your common calendar regardless of whether it is a social event or a bill that must be paid. For example, you need to know when and how you will make bill payments.

You talk about spending limits. Regardless of which partner you select to pay bills or make other money decisions, you decide that you will always consult each other if the price you will pay is over a certain amount. For example, if you are going to pay $250.00 or more for something, you will connect and talk things over first. To consult one another is to honor one another-and it can keep you out of financial trouble

You talk about your budget and what worked and what did not. (There will always be something that doesn't work but remember budgets are about learning.)

This is also the place where you talk about the future. What are your goals? What one thing will both of you save for first in order to get to what you will save for second? Will both of you continue to work or will one of you go back to school? Do you hope to have a baby in the next couple of years? When do you think you will be ready to buy a home? All of these topics are appropriate here.

This is a strategic place where you can decide how your marriage is working and whether it will last. All couples, whether they are conscious of it or not, can easily be competitive. Many couples do not get past the conflict stage in marriage. This is the place where compromise will be necessary.

Here is a what-to-do strategy if your budget planning fails (or maybe even if it does not fail.)

Do not let this come as too big a shock, especially for those of you who live in the world of electronic gadgets. You can learn from how your grandparents and great grandparents did it in the past. They were brilliant and they survived.

So what did they do? They physically took the money and allotted the money to where it was supposed to go. For example, the money in the cookie jar was for school lunches. There were envelopes marked rent/house payment, groceries, car fare/car payment, clothes, and utilities. This made a lot of sense since both knew what money was spent where, and how much. They knew to count up the groceries in the cart and knew how much was in the envelope. They knew impulse buying was out of the question.

People who spend predetermined cash for purchases spend less and usually they also save more. Paying with cash generally is smarter than by check, bank card, or credit card. In short, people who are aware of cash being physically handed over tend to be "richer" in the long run.

11. Move from a savings plan to an investment strategy.

This section may or may not be for you. If you come from a well-to-do family, you may have a financial consultant.

We are now deep enough into strategies that it bears repeating what it is we are doing in this chapter. Millions of people marry without any real investigation of marriage, money, and finances. Money is a major underlying cause of arguments and, of course, divorce. What this chapter is about is laying out a road map, a kind of prescription, that could be followed. Some may find it helpful.

But here is the underlying thought. It is my job to bring up these issues and it is yours to decide what's important and how to act. The intent in this chapter is to bring up enough ideas so that you are empowered to think through the bigger picture of money. It is up to you to check out everything I have said here. That is one of the themes of this book. If you are given enough appropriate information, you will not be afraid to look into these questions together. You together, talking and working things out, is what strengthens your marriage.

Now, choosing people who can guide you into investments is your next task. You were told earlier that it is a good thing to save and work with people you like. This is true also for investment counselors at your credit union, bank, or with an independent company. Like the people you choose to work with. Through friends and people you trust, choose, if you so desire, an advisor to work with. If you are on good terms with your family, consult them for advice as well. When you get a name you think you may go with, check out that person thoroughly.

Banking, whether at your credit union or community bank, for example, may have been where you first saved your emergency fund and you may have started some certificate of deposits, all of them safe and insured by the federal government. You probably have your paycheck automatically deposited to your checking account. You may have started an automatic savings out of your checking account into savings. You may even have a small Christmas club or vacation club account. It would not be unusual to use this place to pay a utility bill automatically.

You now have a choice. Either the two of you are the navigators, the decision makers on your larger investment strategy, or you allow someone else to guide you. Please know that there are a few, more than you might think, investment advisors who would be upset that you did not put your money into an investment level account rather than into your friendly federally insured institution. They shrug off the need for safety and insurance and point out how much more money you might make if you went to a higher level investment even if it is not insured.

If you were doing it on your own, what might you do? Let's say you are really conservative. You might save your emergency fund and keep it federally insured. Then choose the next level which will not necessarily be insured but that will be relatively safe in your mind. This next level will have a return better then you get on your savings but you know you will not make a big killing. The money placed in this might be equal to what your emergency fund is.

Do you see the thinking here? You may feel good about a higher investment level but you are safeguarded because your emergency fund is federally insured. The next riskier level then is safeguarded by the second level of investment which is not federally insured but has a good return record. This approach is a kind of safety pyramid with one level acting as a kind of insurance for the other level(s).

Well, it is interesting that even after what some have called a second depression, stocks have rebounded and people invested in them are doing well again. Most people were afraid of a total economic crash but wiser more mature minds prevailed. So some investments have resiliency.

An example of a second level investment might be a mutual fund based on the Dow Jones Index or a group of very reliable companies. This is not an outright recommendation but is brought to your attention so that you can investigate your possibilities.

Another level of investing is very passive. This one is not necessarily a part of the safety pyramid described earlier. You make a decision once and others do things for you. For example, your employer may tell you that he will give you one dollar for every dollar you put aside in a retirement account. If the boss has money on the line often this can be a good deal. You might join that plan even if you are a newlywed.

Your credit union or bank may offer an automatic small insurance, say a minimum disability type of insurance. If this is the case, be aware of it and know it is a small benefit to you. Check out this kind of thing.

Overall look at insurance carefully. Know that if you have an emergency fund at your bank or credit union, it is a small but effective self-insurance. So I encourage you to take your time and check out other types of insurance. For example, check out the difference between term life insurance and other types of insurance. For people who do not have big incomes, term life insurance may make more sense, especially if the premium is paid automatically every month.

There is more to say about this topic but there are other books for this purpose. By the way, especially if you have an emergency fund in place, you may find that you may not need insurance on children. They are not breadwinners. The first job of life insurance is to insure the income earners.

Living Within Your Means

For new couples something strange can happen early in the relationship. It doesn't have to happen but sometimes it just does. Is this at all familiar to you? It is only strange because most of us have a scarcity mindset. One couple reported to me as follows: "We've been together six months and we are careful with money but each month we are surprised that somehow we have some money left over. Each month it's almost $300."

The amounts some couples have left over can vary. However, this is a kind of window that opens and closes pretty quickly; it does not usually last very long. This is a golden moment. Because of the way so many of us think, we generally do not experience a surplus in money. This situation of a surplus, can and does disappear quickly, especially if you do not do anything about it.

It can be a psychological hurdle to claim that extra money and keep living as if you could do without it. The hurdle often is to get past the idea that you may be doing something wrong. It may also be the fear that if you put the money into savings, you will find yourself in want. Of course if this is the case, this is not your rational self talking; it is your fear talking.

By the way, living this way and saving has a designation-it is called living within your means. And what you can do with this money is always invest it. Invest first in yourself and create an emergency fund. After that you will discover how easily the money can be invested.

Many couples use the surplus money. Opportunity is knocking but they miss their chance. They tell themselves it is okay to spend the money on a want, on a "druther," if you will. If you miss this opportunity, savings and investment will still be doable and still a good thing; but sometimes waiting to save at a later date is also more emotionally challenging.

Money and the Values Challenge

I recently was told by a young fiancé, "I have no values around money. Money is just a thing." Is she naive? Perhaps. She may, however, have learned to say things that people of influence in her life have said. The truth is that money always represents something. There are a myriad of values that go well beyond money simply just being a tool. You will not necessarily know what all your values around money are. You may only be discovering your big money values as your relationship becomes serious and you begin to talk about these things together.

No one can really predict where the two of you will find a money/values conflict. I mean the butting of heads! You will find an impasse at some point. Here is a potential for a large fight that in the long run may not be necessary at all.

There are all kinds of hang-ups including denial and pain avoidance when it comes to talking about money. One of the reasons for avoidance and denial may truly be trauma around the experience of money loss and love loss. Some have found that money can be a sedative for anxiety attacks. This often shows up in a kind of shopping called "retail therapy." Spending money can also be considered to be a process addiction.

Anger around handling money is very common. There is a natural frustration around having your heart set on something only to find your partner has spent that money on something else. There are some few couples who cannot talk and make peace around money issues. They make a bargain that sounds like this. "We'll stay married. But your money will be your money and my money will be my money. We won't mix the money and we will keep separate bank accounts."

This strategy can work to limit bad feelings and arguments. Of course, there is generally a downside as well. It is that you can lose the wisdom of thinking together, and so lose the sense of power of being a real couple together, living out of the same image or similar understanding.

It may be hard for you to let go, share, and work together. There are marriages that work where money is kept separatly or only one person deals with the money. For some, handling money is experienced as a control thing or a power trip. Yet there are others who want to remove themselves from the anxiety of talking and handling money.

Being Prepared for Anger

There are as many points of anger possible with money as there are preconceived notions. There is a reason that this chapter includes communication suggestions and why the preceding chapter is about communication.

As you move deeper into your relationship and your marriage progresses, many of you will cherish the idea of your closeness and romance. You will likely want to keep a sense that you are still best friends and good partners together. So communication about money matters.

One point of anger shows up for many as couples experience loss and financial decline. Job loss, major illness, and investments that have gone bad all contribute to the experience of loss. In particular there can be sadness, anger, and shame because of unemployment. This experience has always existed and always has some impact on marriage. The attitude and relationship you take to it really matters. The idea and emotion of loss and decline is very much in the consciousness of couples everywhere as jobs are lost and countries have moved to the brink of economic depression.

Among the many ways it can be a trigger for anger is that these seemingly overwhelming and/or uncontrollable situations can shatter personal images of what ought to be. One response is to be angry with your partner rather than the underlying condition that is the real cause. Another response is to feel betrayed and give up on your marriage because your partner who was supposed to be the great provider has been brought low by the larger actions taking place in the economy.

It may not seem rational that one partner can feel so much anger that the other has lost his or her role as the leading money earner. This can lead to a so-called "cut and run" response and can be the underlying reason for divorce.

I recommend that you have frank discussions about your relationship to money. I say discussions because most couples find that involvement with money is actually so complex that you will find yourself needing to talk about it a lot. If one of you enjoys dealing with money, it may fall to that one to be compassionate and to help the partner with his or her money struggles. You and your marriage can experience a challenge and you may experience a demand for a greater humanness. Your patience can be severely tested. You may have to help each other heal from this sense of loss.

Long before money struggles appear, even before the formal "I do" is said, in reality you have some sense about yourself as a couple. In fact for many of you there is an experience of being powerfully drawn together. It is almost as if you were already married. In our society we call this the time of engagement. It is the perfect time to discuss and experience how the two of you handle money issues.

Regardless of how you approach money, any time and all the time is a good time to discuss money. Divorce can be financially and emotionally costly. Those couples who can keep their marriages together often find financial success for themselves and can help create financial success for their children.

Creating Your Family Money Philosophy Starter Questions

1. What have you decided about how you will pay your expenses?

2. Who pays the bills and keeps and balances the checkbook? One of you? Both together?

3. Will you have a spending ceiling over which you will not go without consulting the other? $100? $200? $300? Another amount?

4. What are your decisions about where to bank? Credit union? Community bank? Other?

5. What are some of your short-term and long-term goals? Will you set aside 10% for savings? Another amount? Will you have an emergency fund? Are there other goals you can identify?

6. Communication is important, so have you talked about how you will resolve differences and arguments over money?

7. Where will you work on bills, goals, and money questions? Is it the kitchen table? In the den? In the bedroom?

8. How do you get along working together? Have you talked about what it means to create "a safe container" where the two of you can talk? Do you have an agreement to hear each other out?

9. Have you committed to making a budget? Do you know there is no such thing as a perfect budget? Have you decided to learn from this experience?

10. In making goals and planning decisions, have you figured out how to pay for the bigger ticket items?

11. How much do you understand about how savings and checking accounts work? How much bank fees are? How automatic paycheck deposits work? How automatic savings works? How to use certificates of deposit? How and why to have a vacation or holiday club account?

12. Have you identified who can guide you with money questions? Is it your parents? The financial advisor at the Credit Union? Bank? For example, who can explain to you the time-functions of money like, for example, the "sinking fund?"

13. Knowing that heavy debt and credit card use have led to much marriage discord, have you figured out how to manage without a debt load that cuts into your standard of living and quality of life?

14. If you are planning to buy a house, what money do you have to have in place and what will your budget be like?

15. Have you taken advantage of different plans like retirement accounts or matching money for retirement from your employer?

16. What are your long-term savings plans? How does having a baby fit into your budget? Do you want to achieve some sense of financial independence? Are you on the same page when it comes to your priorities?

Chapter **8**

Relationships with Relatives

 I successfully negotiate marriage challenges
to build lasting intimacy.

Chapter 8

*T*here are many roles and benefits for married couples in interacting with their relatives. Here are a few.

Family as tradition: Ideally there are several functions that extended family members play. They help you continue practices and traditions that are the cultural fabric of your family. That is the say, they help create a way to more fully celebrate life.

Family as a mirror: Your larger family also is a mirror to you of what is working in your relationship. It reflects back to you your own importance and validates the functioning of your family. Someone or some others must always play this mirroring role and good friends do it naturally without being told. Extended family members can also be ideal.

Family as friendships: The relationships of all of family young and old, cousins, aunts, uncles, and grandparents enrich our lives. They offer a sense of connection and belonging.

Family as nurture and care: Although many families today are geographically distant from one another, the nurture that, for example, grandparents can give grandchildren is often missing. Grandparents can be emotionally healing for their grandchildren-especially when frustrated parents have too much to do and cannot focus all of the necessary attention on their kids.

Family as leadership and community building: This is too often a little discussed, and little understood, family function. However, families do not thrive without participation in community. For you as couple and for your extended family, community-sustaining activities will always be a part of your marriage. This is a more powerful experience when you and your relatives engage in these things together. Whether it is an activity like a walk to end hunger or supporting Little League or participating in neighborhood cleanup, your marriage and family engagement in community are required.

As I think you may understand, however, connecting with some family members is generally supportive and joyful, while connecting with others is a downer or occasionally even dangerous. Marital fights often occur about how to connect with in-laws in particular and which ones to listen to. Sometimes it can be the in-laws that instigate fights between the two of you.

The question can become, who in your family can you trust? It is important to get these relationships right because they can really offer support to you as a couple and, furthermore, these are the same people that will be the elders and even grandparents to your children. If it is not possible to have good relationships with your parents (in-laws), than like millions of other couples you may have to forego these interactions. This can be a hard decision and can change the quality of your marriage for better or worse.

There are critical decisions about which relatives you love "at a distance," which relatives need to be separated from your nuclear family, and ways to deal with those who are troublesome. So you inevitably will ask yourself: How does extended family support work? Will you be involved in a multigenerational family situation? There is no one right way, so it is a question of how will it work best for you.

Just because someone is related to you does not mean that this person is a friend. Perhaps you have a domineering mother-in-law who insists that every holiday will be run her way. Or how about the sleazy uncle who hits on anyone in a skirt? Or, conversely, the aunt who is a perpetual flirt? The problems relatives bring to your marriage can come from both male and female relatives and can vary widely in kind.

In this chapter we will help you and encourage the two of you to strategize approaches to difficult family relationships. Family relationships are too often the source of dissension and argument for many couples.

The Dilemma of Bad Relationships

A couple of factors make this a difficult subject. First, problematic relatives may have genuine gifts for you, your spouse, and for your own family. In weighing the negative side of relatives, especially in-laws, the gifts of kindness, support, and love should not be summarily dismissed. Second, your emotional tie, a strong love bond, to your relatives may not easily be put aside.

One of the most serious complaints is about unwarranted in-law interference in your marriage. This may come from the husband's over-protective parents who are consumed with the idea that a new fiancé or wife will not appropriately take care of her son. The same attitude can be true for parents of the daughter. "This guy is just not good enough for our girl," they may say.

Sometimes in-laws cannot give up their perceived ownership of their now-grown child and meddle so much in a new relationship that they are the source of a crisis. This is an extreme but not uncommon situation. The meddling can be a chief factor in dividing you and creating unnecessary arguments. This kind of interference can only go on for so long. You may discount the problem by going along to get along. You may even tolerate your partner's soft-heartedness for his or her parents. After all, they do deserve respect and love.

One person in my practice discussed his relationship to his father. The following story is not uncommon, and I have had several clients with similar experiences. "When I was growing up I was always severely criticized. I lived in fear of my dad both because he was a harsh critic and because he would freely hit me when he was angry." The story continues: "Today my father has somewhat mellowed, but when I saw him chew out my own son, I spoke to him. He didn't get it and there were several more instances. I broke off my relationship with my dad to protect my son. It seems the whole family turned on me and I have little contact with most of my family."

This is a courageous act and stops a pattern that is damaging. The son certainly loved his dad but he could not allow his dad's wounds to be projected onto his own son.

Parents for Good or Strife?

Parents can interfere with your family to the point where it causes arguments between the two of you. When it comes to overbearing interference, my suggestion to you is that outside interference from relatives cannot be allowed to trump your relationship with each other. Your parents and your relatives are important but not more important than your spouse! You as a couple are much better off discussing your families now rather than having problems sneak up on you.

Parents exhibit real leadership in some families. When responsible parents set the tone of integrity and fairness, everyone in the family circle can experience positive benefits. For example, when a matriarch or patriarch is known for tolerance, calm reflection, and integrity, usually the family as a whole is likely to express a supportive loving kindness to one another. The good influence of elders often can and does translate into good family relationships.

Many families benefit from the good leadership of their elders. Even so, many families have to deal with other serious relationship questions. For example, there are many families, more than you might think, that must deal with mentally ill relatives. What do you do when a close family member is "crazy"?

Mental Illness as a Challenge

You may or may not know that this is not an isolated question that only affects you. This question is not just for the family. The question of how to deal with someone's mental illness is being raised in schools, workplaces, and the various institutions that influence our daily lives. The answer is not always simple.

Here is one perspective that can help. When a relative exhibits unusual or wild behavior that is not a threat to you or your loved ones, this family member deserves support and consideration. Your help and understanding may be needed. Being supportive and helpful in getting help for your relative and standing by them can be the compassionate thing to do. What may help you to arrive at this decision is that you and your spouse are not perfect and that both of you carry baggage. It can give you a place of authentic caring for a sick relative.

However, there are mental conditions that can be a threat to you and your family. The most serious are illnesses or disorders that lead to criminal behavior. In this situation, when someone who is related to you has a mental condition that involves a threat or an implied threat to your safety, I recommend that you do everything it takes to distance yourself. While getting help for this relative is important as well, this recommendation cannot be overstated. Especially if you have children, do not expose them to physically and verbally violent family members. If one of your relatives tries to involve you in social arrangements that include a dangerous family member, you need to not be roped into that social occasion.

You as a couple have no choice but to decide how to deal with your relatives. Sometimes you know that they are surely nuts and being with them feels like watching a circus. Often arguments and later divorce center on the complaints and divisiveness that relatives can cause. This situation can cause a real dilemma because both spouses have to decide on what action is appropriate.

It Takes Three to Make a Couple

According to some therapists, married couples need at least one other person who can give support and understanding to the struggle of marriage. Normally someone related to the couple plays this role. However, if family members are not appropriate for this role, it is a bit harder to find anyone who fills the bill. However, a mutual friend could play this role. You may not be aware, but every couple needs a third person that sees them as a family and gives some support and advice. In this sense, the sense of legitimate friendship and mirroring, a married couple is three people. Observers find marriages can deteriorate without this kind of support.

The all-important supportive mirroring function of a third person may have largely disappeared from the American scene. This is true because many relatives are separated by miles and live many states away. It is also true because we don't often know the people in our own neighborhood and don't have positive relationships with them. In other words, most of the rest of us don't do an effective job in supportively relating to the married couples in our sphere of influence.

However, not getting enough outside support is not as serious as negative inputs from relatives that are destructive to you. It is a serious problem when relatives want to project their own baggage onto one of you or onto your marriage in general. These can come from negative roles that you can do without. They can include, for example, the controlling, the know-it-all, the jealous, the perpetually offended, and the drunk relative.

These situations can be perplexing and even emotionally upsetting. Some of you may reflect on your parents and relatives and ask, "What do you do when my family member that is supposed to love me simply doesn't?" Maybe you feel the sting of rejection and feel abandoned. Yet there is good news. This is exactly one reason that you have found someone you love, your spouse, your husband or wife, who loves you. It is up to you to stop the hurt and division that negative family influences have created. You can do it.

The Inevitable Wound

Here is another truth you should consider when thinking through your relationships with your parents. Every parent wounds his or her children in one way or another. There are no exceptions. I have met some who vehemently deny that their parents wounded them. In reality there are no exceptions. If the two of you become parents you will no doubt be loving and nurturing. And yet the two of you, possibly inadvertently, will wound your children.

For some this realization is tough to get. Some people come from a powerful tradition that prohibits any public family criticism whatsoever. Getting beyond your own somewhat hazardous growing up wounds is important to create a good relationship with your parents and with your children. While this chapter is about information that could help you protect your marriage from undue and divisive family negativity, not all couples face the same family problems. Some families are very loving and protective. However no set of parents is perfect. Even the best families create problematic situations and children can easily be hurt as they take these in.

It is a good thing that most families are helpful to each other. This help can be wide ranging and may even, for example, include sharing their home as you get stable in your own relationship. You may likewise be of great help and support to them as your marriage is established. It is a two-way street.

Identify Your Values for Family Relationships Starter Questions

1. When you get married, where will you live? Will it be with your family, or will you live on your own?

2. Do you come from an old-fashioned multi-generational set of connections, and do you want to create that kind of home? Or will you be a nuclear family starting with just the two of you?

3. How does how you grew up relate to your proposed living environment?

4. Will you have supportive family relationships, or will you have to distance from your families in order to be protected and stay sane?

5. Do you have a common set of traditions and understandings with your relatives? What are they?

6. Even in healthy families there are problems. Have you discussed how to handle slights and belittlements from parents or other relatives? What do each of you need to understand?

7. If your respective families are competitive and require you to be present at all of their holiday functions, have you discussed how to resolve these demands? What are some solutions?

8. Have you discussed how talking about family affects you? Is it positive or negative? If it creates negativity, how might you work better together?

9. How might you handle these kinds of pressure? Do the two of you simply give in to family pressure, going along to get along?

10. Have you identified the family members who stand up for you and like you as a married couple? Who are they? Have you expressed gratitude for their support?

11. If you are planning to have children, have you discussed the roles grandparents might play in the lives of your kids? What roles would your mother and father play in the lives of your kids? What roles would they not play?

Tree of Sun
This is the symbol for planting well and establishing strong roots. It seeks the powerful light of truth as it reaches for the illuminating and purifying sunlight.

May the sober and realistic promises you make
to one another bring light to you;
may they be the grounding roots
of towering love and abiding intimacy.

Part 3

Creating Your New Life Story
in Four Covenants

This is the best time, during the time of your engagement or early marriage, to begin shaping your ideas of how you will be as a couple and as a family. For those of you who are newlyweds, revisiting the topics in this part of the book can serve to strengthen your relationship.

This section is about the four covenants of marriage. The couple's work around sex, communication, money, and in-laws is important. The work of making agreements, covenants, and creating a foundational relationship between the two of you is also important. This second kind of work combines knowledge about solving marriage's biggest problems with laying a rational and spiritual relationship for your marriage.

These chapters have good and powerful work for you. This section is not only for those who are engaged, newly married, and, yes, even those who are living together and not married. Even if you have not taken a step to the altar, you will be surprised at how many agreements the two of you have made about how you do things together.

You will find the next chapters will require thoughtfulness. All of the information you have noted down before about how you met, what your history has been, who your family is, how you are alike and different, etc., is foundational and now gets utilized in these chapters.

Here you talk about how your family will take shape. So, for the sake of argument, let's say you might come to a place where you won't know what to say. My suggestion is to guess at what is needed. It is better for you to risk saying something and working with it later than not to say anything, leave, and miss something important. Some of you may be afraid to risk ideas about the future.

The key is to have fun and risk a little!

Chapter 9

Making Promises to Keep: Knowing and Owning the Marriage Covenant

I am creating, knowing and living
my covenant to my relationship,
strengthening my marriage.

Chapter 9

*T*his is the part where you say "I do" in public. Here we look at the public covenant, the one you make "before God and everybody." It may be religious or secular, but it is the formal commitment. It also involves your decision to build a conscious trust relationship with your significant other.

The public "I dos" are a beginning. However, trust is built as you solve problems and make joint decisions. The more you are involved in discussing your marriage, the stronger your marriage is likely to be.

These two ideas are the underlying themes in this book. You are opening your eyes to the challenges of marriage. As you read it, no doubt most of you still feel a powerful romantic connection. This is a gift. It is the "loving feeling" that can motivate this personal work and therefore enrich your marriage and bring you more intimacy.

Love indeed is about promises. It is a kind of "I promise you" scenario. You may also have looked into each others' eyes saying words like "I don't ever want to lose you. You are so important to me." That is the place where romance and promises get verbalized. Let's explore what they mean.

The promises of love send the heart racing and the mind swirling. Imaginations grow bold with a vision of caring, kind loving and a healing future. The first taste of love is usually delicious. Experiencing special moments with your lover can be thrilling and healing. No wonder lovers want to continue their love connection into the future. And making vows is about keeping love alive into the future. Most couples hope the thrill, affirmation, and validation that they have found in one another will continue.

Couples commit to marriage, plan a wedding, invite important people, take vows, and exchange rings in the hopes of keeping alive the best of what they have found in each other. However, with time, your focus will begin to shift. In the space which is your life, you will need to make room for work, housekeeping, maintaining friendships, and so many other things. Often the focus becomes all the roles you play rather than just the excitement of being in love.

There is a reason to bring up your romantic feelings. These feelings can provide time and energy to give you a kind of buffer zone in which you get to know each other better. It is also a great time to make decisions together. For many, the romantic drive matures sometime before the third year of your relationship. Then, all of the things you shared, the truth telling, the working out of problems, and the trust building can really pay off. You will be entering a new phase of your love life.

It Is Appropriate to Make the Love Decision

So that is the place where marriage, the marriage ceremony, and the vows come in. In toasting and giving advice to a new couple, a wise person once said at a community (aka rehearsal or congregation) dinner, "Don't depend on your love to make your marriage work. Depend on your marriage to make your love work." Too many people do the first thing only, and it can screw up their marriages.

This section is about creating the foundations that make marriage work and therefore expand and strengthen your intimacy and love life. Formally, it starts with the decision to say the first "I do." What you hopefully will learn is that besides your beautiful romantic experience, love is a decision. Besides your emotions, love is thoroughly and completely pure decision. With luck, you will often experience the romance as well as the work of building a love relationship that is grounded in ever-greater maturity.

You may realize that you are two authentic people who belong together. You may also realize that in everything you do for each other and together, you are building your love connection. You may come to know that people (you) don't just simply fall out of love because things change--because you will learn that you didn't just simply fall in love. And, of course, for some people the word "falling" means an accident. You may believe that you fell in love, and that's great. But there is really more to it than what is described by the word "falling."

As you work together, your compatibility and achievements may give you a more rational perspective. You may even come to celebrate a deeper understanding that your relationship was meant to be. Your relationship is the right one for you. You may also learn that as you did not simply "fall" in love, so you will not simply "fall" out of love.

And that is why covenants matter. The public covenant sets the intention and path of your relationship. You know that this public covenant invites the community, in fact the whole world, to recognize, honor, and support your marriage. Because our cultural view of the public marriage covenant is somewhat fractured and understood in piecemeal, in this part we discuss the covenant knowing it is one, but also as four covenants. One covenant is symbolic for many different parts of your relationship and implies a lot more than is said in words.

Hopefully you will know that the person-your lover, your best friend-with whom you share the most intimate secrets and with whom you reach for the most fulfilling of life's goals, is the one you decided to love. Understanding and realizing this, that love is decision, is a big key to maintaining a successful marriage.

Just because you have a covenant does not mean that you will always agree. Couples arguing is not usually a pretty sight. The anger needs to be said. Without delineating it in so many words, the marriage covenant commits the two of you to a relationship in which you use anger constructively. You will both get angry but how you relate to it matters. When you come to an impasse as all couples do and when emotions run high, the work you do here can make all the difference in the world.

What is important is the intention and spirit with which you decide to be with each other. Vows are about saying what you will do and doing what you say. If that does not happen, then you will need to take responsibility for what you did or did not do. It is this stance of integrity that is a part of the vows you take.

Vows are a way of affirming a covenant with each other. Many traditional vows are beautiful and meaningful. Some couples find a cleric who will accept the use of self-written vows. Most couples, however, mainly worry about saying their responses right and getting through the wedding ceremony.

Working Out the Personal Meanings of Marriage
Starter Questions

1. If you have decided where and by whom you will be married, have you read the vows and discussed what they mean to you?

2. What do the vows mean to each of you? How is your love reflected in your vows and ceremony?

3. How do you understand the friendship between the two of you?

4. As you get set to take these public vows, say in your own words what your marriage is about. In other words, what is the meaning of marriage to you?

5. The marriage vows are also about honoring each other. How do you understand the word "honoring"? How have you experienced it and what does it mean to each of you?

6. Discuss loyalty, fidelity, and integrity. How do you think these ideas will play out in your relationship?

7. In your relationship, what role has accountability played thus far? How are you accountable to each other?

8. What is your experience in forgiving others and being forgiven? Discuss forgiveness in your relationship.

9. What are some of the larger goals and agreements you have as you enter this covenant? Discuss these in some detail and discuss what might happen if the goals don't work out or if one of you changes his or her mind.

10. Before taking the vows, have you discussed whether you want to have children? What role will children play in your marriage?

Chapter 10

Marriage's Intimacy Challenge: Creating Your Personal Sex Covenant

 I am creating, knowing and living
my covenant to my relationship,
strengthening my marriage.

Chapter *10*

*I*n this chapter we revisit the topic of sex again. This time it is not to talk about physical compatibility. Instead, in this chapter we will discuss how partner relationships may work in a marriage. In the last chapter we talked about the public covenant. In this one the topic is the private, sexual covenant.

Being together, you experience the joys of sharing. It is not just about the person you are but the person that you will be, the person you will become. There is a lot to being present in your relationship. Being together is often about being romantic, doing with one another the little things that mean a lot. These things like holding hands, caressing, hugging, whispering your hopes and dreams to one another, touching, having a candlelit meal are all part of what makes romance, love, and sex work.

Usually, as you learn about how to be more compatible and to be one another's partner, you also begin to learn how sex with one another works. As we noted earlier in the book, many of you may already be sexually intimate. However, no one person's experience or background will be the same. For many of you there may have been no earlier preparation for physical intimacy. Sex ed may only consist of being told to maintain abstinence or always use a condom.

At this point, as a serious couple, you begin to see how sex improves romance, love, and health. At least, intuitionally you begin to realize that sex, besides being fun, changes and enhances everything in your relationship. It can be breathtaking to grasp how important sex is. Besides the point that sex is really great, it is necessary to talk out your sexual thinking, ask questions about what each partner needs, and decide what your sexual relationship and responsibilities to one another are.

For the most part there are no words about a couple's sex life in their marriage vows. At the point of taking vows, the questions about your future do not necessarily revolve around your sexual experience. They do, however, revolve around questions of the mutual role of fidelity, that is, faithfulness, in your marriage.

In good and troubled times, at the very core of your relationship, there is the question of how dependable your care is for each other. For most of you, sex is at the heart of how the two of you will be together. No one, though, can fully predict what a couple's sex life will be. Will it be robust or will it be a bust? You can begin to decide now because what you think and what you want can be really important. You can re-decide later as needed and, so to speak, flow with the roller coaster of life.

If you are engaged or newly married, you have had a lot of conversations about sex. This may or may not be new ground to cover for you.

The power of sex is not ever really addressed within the public marriage covenant. In marriage, sex is powerfully life-enhancing. Most of you will often have differing views of sex. If you have had sexual relations as a single, you may know that sometimes sex before the marriage relationship can be disappointing, and can even be scary. Also, without being in a committed relationship, it can be worrying to have sex with someone not knowing whether your immediate partner has had sex with others who may have had a sexually transmitted disease.

The private, sexual covenant does not usually come together at once but is a result of many conversations. Therefore, the first sexual covenant is usually a verbal one. For your own sake, and for clarity, it is helpful to write out what your sexual relationship is, and what it is you want to learn about together. This is not for public consumption but can be a part of your own Couple's Book. Naturally your own thinking and agreements will be somewhat different from other's agreements.

Creating the Sense of a Personal Covenant Starter Questions

1. Here is a key question for committed couples: have the two of you discussed what you mean by loyalty, faithfulness, and trust?

2. What do you expect sexually from each other? What can you agree on?

3. Some couples go into marriage having had some good sex with each other, but not really understanding what the other hopes for. What do each of you hope to get out of your sexual relationship over time?

4. What obligations and responsibilities do you have to each other?

5. What happens when one of you needs sexual attention and the other is lukewarm or not interested?

6. Have you discussed different ways of being sexual? Language, touch, positions, fantasies? (Suggestion: even if this is more than one conversation, take the time to follow up.)

7. Do you both understand each other's likes and each other's boundaries? What is your understanding of being sexual? How do you talk about being sexual? How might it be reflected in your marriage?

8. What words describe for you, your sexual understanding with each other? (Suggestion: for the sake of clarity, write these out.)

9. Do you both understand what your sexual commitment to each other is? (Suggestion: if not, go over what you remember about your earlier discussions and/or notes.)

10. Have you decided whether your sexual covenant will be strictly verbal or whether, just for clarity's sake, it will be written? If written, decide if it will be in the form of bullet points or in paragraph form.

Chapter 11

A Covenant of Marriage Organization and Union: Your Family Constitution and What It Takes to Be Successful!

 I am creating, knowing and living
my covenant to my relationship,
strengthening my marriage.

Chapter 11

Compatibility. You are in love and you are likely feeling the joy. You now have a strong sense of your compatibility. Life does get more complicated. In day-to-day living, the stress creators--making a household, building your careers, having a family--all consume your focus. The special things about you and your relationship can get lost. I presume that you want to be together to keep and enjoy the very best you have found in each other. So it is important to do some thinking about how you would like to be as a couple.

A lot of couples cannot and often do not figure out how to do things together and are involved in ongoing battles. You may not happen to avoid that dreaded conflict stage of marriage but you shorten and resolve it more easily when you work out this covenant. Of course, this book is about thinking and learning how to work together. So taking this idea one step farther, the family constitution is really thinking and learning how you can work out your problems together.

In this chapter we will focus on two different things. First, I will share some ideas on emotional and intellectual intelligence and compatibility and, second, on creating the family constitution so that hopefully it works for you.

You know, of course, some very bright people with high intelligence scores are often unable to maintain good relationships. It is surprising. Then there are others, those people who understand emotions and get along very well with others, but who are not oriented to practical tasks like balancing the checkbook. The point I want to make is that, while people vary a lot, you have the choice to use your various gifts together or you can let them come to divide you.

The more you know about the nature of your feelings and get clear that your emotions and decisions need to match in some way with each other, the stronger your marriage will likely be. The more you can bring your intellectual understanding to the practical tasks at hand, the more likely your family will operate better. While developing a strong emotional intelligence is important, so is paying the mortgage on time.

Also, there will come times when you will need your partner to understand where you are coming from-to understand not only what your thinking is but also what you are feeling. Engagement and marriage are not times for pretense to impress your partner. You should not have to put on an act and therefore hide the person you really are.

Speaking your truth and being able to listen to your partner's truth will go a long way toward building a powerful and intimate relationship. Usually strong marriages create a feeling of acceptance, validation, and well-being. This kind of relationship also tends to bring about a level of financial security. The opposite tends to be true for emotionally unhappy couples, and emotionally unhappy couples often experience arguments which create a kind of emotional poverty.

Continuous emotional battles drain a lot of energy and hijack creative thinking. Bickering and fighting can weaken a marriage and also begin to limit economic possibilities. These battles can also destroy trust and loyalty, so that chances of creating or building real intimacy are damaged.

Marriage roles vary. They include supporting one another not just when times are good but also when there are challenges such as times when one or both get sick or lose a job. Of course, one couple's successful marriage will look different than another couple's.

There are some criteria to measure success. Among them are:
- being happy,
- being able to talk to each other (including about money), and
- experiencing trust and well-being as you relate to each other.

In a strong marriage losing a job and becoming poor does not mean the end of the marriage. In the history of this country and the history of the world, millions of people have been poor but have had what might be considered good marriages.

Your marriage and how you think about it does not have to match or live up to someone else's view of marriage. How you relate to your partner and problems also has everything to do with what intelligence you will bring to writing the family constitution.

Getting to the How of How You Make It Work as a Couple Starter Questions

1. What do you think of when you think of a happy marriage?

2. When you see a happy marriage, what is it that you are seeing?

3. What does being together mean to you? Specifically, what has changed for you now that you are together? How are you different than when you were single?

4. As you have been spending time together, what are some things you have already learned from each other?

5. You are probably aware love changes over time. How has it changed since you first realized you loved each other?

6. What are your interests and hobbies? Which do you share? Which ones do you do alone?

7. Are your interests compatible with having a marriage partner in your life? What would be a goal or interest that could tear up your marriage?

8. What are your ideas about romance? What activities are romantic for both of you?

9. How do you plan to keep romance alive? Specifically, how will you handle the question of making time for each other? (Will your time together continue? Will you date each other even when you are married? If so, how frequently? On what day?)

10. Are each of you able to forgive? If so, when was the last time you forgave one another? What did you say? If not, how can you begin to practice forgiveness?

11. When has a fight created a temporary rift between the two of you? Do the two of you know how to fight fairly? How would you define a fair fight?

12. Hopefully the two of you are able to speak your truth. What is the toughest part of speaking your own truth?

13. How well do you work together now? If you both get along, can you articulate what it is you do that allows you to work together?

14. In your life experience, where have you found yourself working in team situations or in high collaboration? What is it from those experiences that you can bring to family life?

15. Make a list of all of the practical things you can do in the setting up of your daily marriage. Think about things like cooking, cleaning, bookkeeping, maintaining the household, and painting. What does this tell you about how you want to do things in your marriage?

Writing the Family Constitution

Our famous United States Constitution starts with the words, "We the people . . ." The two of you are the people in this marriage. How will you do it together? What are some important guidelines for you? Everyone will have family constitutions that are both similar and different. If you are wondering what might make up a family constitution, you can look at this suggested outline:

Preamble: Forming a Partnership in Love with Trust and Fidelity

I. Our Financial Guidelines: The Who, What, and Where of Making Our Money and Family Work

II. Financial Partners in Good Times and Bad: What Guides Us in Making Decisions and How It Is We Give Steadfast Support to Each Other

III. Our Family Decision Making, The Partner Meeting, The Family Meeting, and Individual Responsibilities

IV. The Family Mission, Keeping the Faith, Relating to Relatives and Friends, and Supporting Community

V. Raising Children: Partner Collaboration, Responsibilities, and Discipline

VI. Problem Solving, Decision Making, and Forgiveness

Note that the outline above may be different than what you decide on. First, talk this out. Second, refer to notes you have created as you went through this book. Make notes about what is important to you, take some courage, and jump in!

Background to Help Your Writing

How strong is your relationship? How willing are you to risk getting this done? The family constitution, a covenant that you create together, can never work unless the two of you have a strong personal relationship.

In the previous section you were asked about your compatibility and interests. You were also asked how you fight and how it is you speak your truth. In order to write a family constitution, it is helpful for the two of you to have some sense of how you are together.

Take time to reflect on all of the work you have completed so far. Some of your work may represent your best intuitions. If so, you are not alone. Many couples have made their best decisions using intuition.

If intuition plays a part in what you write down, that's okay. What is important is that you have done the best you know how. Whether you are totally sure about how well you have done the previous work, the real question here is not whether you are perfect. It is more about a deeper consideration. It is about whether you feel good about each other and trust each other.

If you have done your best and you have experienced good discussions with each other, then you are ready to write a family constitution. A constitution is a terrific document for couples because it offers the possibility of an overview and summary of what each of you understand and believe. I encourage you to do it … now.

Create your constitution now. Decide the main topics and jump into it. Don't be afraid to rewrite it once or twice. There are no starter questions for this exercise. Remember the following: getting it done is better than having it perfect. You are a compatible couple and if you find you need to change something later there will be time for that. Everyone's constitution is a set of guidelines but also a work in progress. One hint: for some couples it is easier to make a set of bullet point statements rather than writing whole paragraphs. Sometimes bullet points are easier to re-organize.

Chapter 12

Creating a Family Covenant of Service

I am creating, knowing and living
my covenant to my relationship,
strengthening my marriage.

Chapter *12*

*W*e have discussed the public vows you take as a couple and the private vows, particularly the sexual covenant, and the covenant of family organization, the family constitution.

Every family makes a place for itself in a community. It is a kind of "footprint." Every person and every family has the choice to be conscious or unconscious about what kind of family they are, and what as a family they stand for, and what it is they do.

What kind of marriage and family you are and what it is you do goes to the heart of your family identity. Whether you are conscious or unconscious about your family identity, it shapes how you relate to everyone else and how they relate to you. The clearer you are about understanding yourself and your stance in relation to the community at large, the more likely you are to have a healthy and successful marriage.

There is a powerful truth to be recognized in this discussion. It is always in the background of marriage and family reality. Families that ignore participation in community activities and some kind of service usually diminish their quality of life. The neighborhood and community also decline. This is not just true for you but it is also true everywhere in the world. Community is the challenge of our time.

The family covenant of service has two parts, both of which are framed as missions: a personal mission and family mission. Mission was once a term relegated to the military or to the church. Today the word mission is very common. It is not unusual that people, families, organizations, and businesses have missions.

There are two steps to creating this the covenant of service. The first is for each of you to formalize your own mission alone and in dialogue with each other; the second is to write out your family mission together. So what is it you stand for and what is it you do as individuals and as a family?

Many people and couples already have a sense about basic values like honesty, fairness, charity, love, and service to others. Of course, how you approach basic values is unique to the two of you. Unless one or both of you are totally greedy people, you have some values that can lend themselves to a personal mission. With those personal mission values clarified, you will also then grasp your family mission more easily.

Creating Your Mission as a Couple Starter Questions

1. Take time to brainstorm your beliefs. What are they?

2. What life values, principles, or beliefs do you stand for?

3. Are your personal beliefs compatible with your partner's? Take time to discuss both beliefs and goals.

4. How will you work out differences between the two of you? Take time to discuss both details and philosophy.

5. Who do you know in public life or personally, who has translated their beliefs into a mission? List these people you admire.

6. What is it you admire about other people's missions?

7. Who do you know specifically that has a family mission? Extend your research to families outside of your immediate circle. Which friends give you clues about families that seem to have a mission?

8. You may be on your own writing a mission statement. So again, have you talked to each other about your deepest desires and goals? Is there a noble cause in which you both believe that is greater than yourselves?

9. What is it that brings you bliss, serves others, or is your deepest heart's desire?

Facing the Major Challenging Arenas of Relationship Together

Here are some reflective thoughts to let you think about your mission. Compare and reflect on your answers as you read this.

Perhaps your ideas have not been given voice and may be unclear. Maybe the two of you have not really discussed what your big hopes, beliefs, and dreams are. You may be able to create the beliefs and statements about your mission from what you already know. Sometimes help is available from your very sharp, conscientious friends, or family members.

Another way of thinking about this topic is to ask what each of you stand for as individuals. What is it you agree to stand for together? What, then, do you think your family is about and what does your family stand for?

The circumstances in which we live can sometimes provide the context for a mission. For example, having to deal with tragedies, illnesses, and accidents can challenge a family to a whole different level of missional thinking.

There are numerous examples of this. 1. Parents who undertake an effort to help all handicapped children because they have been awakened by having a handicapped child. 2. A person who has alcohol illness may include attention to personal treatment and provide treatment for others as part of their mission.

Some great noble missions are simply undertaken because it is the right thing for a person and a family to do. Other missions are thrust upon them and are so substantial that there is no escaping it.

However, just one person alone can never accomplish a great mission. It certainly takes family support. More than that, a great mission takes interacting and collaborating with a large number of people.

One such example of a mission that is forced upon most people may also come as a surprise to you. It has to do with living in community. Community has everything to do with writing a family mission.

Geographic communities are in flux as more and more people move in and out. The stable, small-town geographic community still exists and is functional in some places. However, in reality, people in suburbs and cities often live very separate lives. It is true that the majority of the world's population now live in cities. Many of them have arrived in cities because their old villages and neighborhoods are in upheaval. Ethnic communities become dispersed. Kinfolk find themselves in distant geographies. Cultural traditions are often in turmoil and flux.

Well, maybe you think you already know what community is for you. If you do, your thinking and wisdom will be helpful to your family. However, it is not surprising that couples are challenged to identify community, figure out how to belong to a community, and also how to build community. What community is and how it works is the great social question of our time.

Most people yearn for a sense of community and most families have a need to identify with community. Community can be based on geography, institutions, and interests, and be globally interconnected. It can be mixture of many things. However, it must function to sustain both adults and children. Today, in the many places we call home, we are lucky if we even know our neighbors or have any strong, meaningful identity of place. We are fortunate if people in our own neighborhood are really our friends.

It is clear that one of the jobs families have is to create and build community. You might include this in thinking about mission. Community is one place to start thinking about mission. It will be a continuous challenge. How else can you really start thinking about mission and service?

Just a word about partner interaction: please do not force your own mission on your partner and don't force what you think is a good mission on each other.

A Brief Personal Mission Workshop

Have you heard this saying? "Every person needs work to do, people to love, and a noble cause greater than themselves to believe in." If the people you love and the work you do is connected to your sense of values and to your personal faith, then you have a beginning way to articulate your mission.

The above saying also reflects the possibility that true fulfillment is derived from your efforts not only to serve yourself or your family, but also to make a difference in your larger community and the world.

On a large sheet of scratch paper, please write things down as you read these next explanations:

Let your intuition guide you to what your ideas of personal mission are. Then discuss them with your partner.
Example: The way I want to be is ... I am a leader for (of) ... I am an advocate of ... My particular gift is ...

Second, look at where your heart's desire or life passion is. Does this fit with who you really are and what you have said so far?

Third, write out your own personal mission. Dream a little ahead. Look five or ten years into the future and ask what it is you believe and what you need to be about. Get an answer. How does that fit with what you have written so far?

Then reflect for yourself whether this truly fits with what your dreams and hopes really are. Picture yourself as the little boy or the little girl that you are in your memory. Does what you have said about your mission help your little boy or girl? Can you see your little girl or boy cheering for your mission? Does this mission serve the wisdom, hopes, and memories of your childhood that are so precious and important to you? Will your inner child jump for joy?

All you need to do now is add action to the statement above-that is, if there is no action in your statement already. Usually the words of action are something like "by doing such and such." For example: "By serving ... ," "By designing ... ," "By speaking my truth ..."

Your mission can be a very simple statement. It does not have to be complicated. A minister friend's is simple: "I bless others as I have been blessed." Another simple one to get you started: "I share my vision of whole-hearted living by asking for help, so that I may also help others."

Another example, a little more complex: "I live my compassion and generosity by giving to and helping others in need, to create a more generous and compassionate world." Another example: "I am a leader for healing and an advocate for peace. My healing mission is to create freedom by speaking my truth to allow all people to find themselves and be themselves." One final example: "My mission is to bring prosperity to members of my community through my coaching and teaching so that I may positively enrich 10,000 lives."

You begin to get the idea. Remember that your personal mission is unique. It is your vision or dream simply said, it is your action, and it is your outcome.

If you have come this far, you have done a tremendous job. The family mission will now be very much easier. If you have not already, do start writing for yourself, do start and finish as best you can. Don't worry about how complete it might be. Once you have a mission statement roughed out in draft form, take it to your partner. Remember, for those of you who are perfectionists: your mission statement does not have to be totally right. Do not go for absolutely perfect.

A Brief Family Mission Workshop

Now you can write your family mission. Think through your ideas and then discuss them with your partner. What are common values and mission interests for you? These can also be simply stated.

Usually there is an internal piece to the family; this piece has to do with nurture and love for one another. There is an external piece which expresses how you are as a family have a positive effect on your community and world. You see, as you love, nurture, and serve each other in your family, you inevitably reflect those qualities onto your greater family, and onto your community and world.

Your mission could be as simple as two or three sentences. It could be one paragraph-or if you have thought a lot about it, it could be a couple of paragraphs. For the external piece start with how your gifts impact others. If that is enough, then you are done with your family mission.

If there is more, write that out as well. For example, you may have passions, goals, dreams, and gifts you share as a family. The two of you may agree on a goal of passion. Your goals will be different from those of other families.

Here is an example: your passion could be ending hunger in the world. This is a huge idea but a worthy and noble goal. (This is a great noble deed that you cannot do by yourself, but you can as a part of a larger network, which is a very valuable mission.) Besides, in the work you have with the internal and external piece you may have already written this kind of thing; if so it can also be a big part of the mission you write.

Think about what you stand for and what it is you would then see. Again do these things serve you and do the outcomes serve others? Does it build community?

Each person, as individuals and family, shows up with gifts and with a mission, conscious or unconscious. Every family has, and somehow is, a gift to the larger world. Let your creative juices flow. All family mission statements will be unique and different. Some will be short and some will be long. Please do not stress out because you have not said something absolutely perfectly. Ultimately mission statements guide and inform but they are never absolutely perfect.

The three examples below may help you.

The Miller Family Mission Statement

We are Maria, Thomas, John, and Susan, the Miller family.

Our family mission is to love one another, to sustain each other, to be strong as individuals and strong as a family. We care for each other, we worship together, and we serve ourselves and others sharing the love which we nurture in our family.

Our family models authentic and whole-hearted living so that we can fully embrace our lives and model the love and authenticity we want to see in our world. We take responsibility for the education of children and as adults we commit to lifelong learning ourselves.

In our service to others we call on the traditions of our parents and grandparents who struggled as farmers in hard times. Therefore as a family we embrace service to end the desperation of want from hunger so that with our efforts, joining with others, the world might be fed.

The Ozols Family Mission Statement

Our family nurtures the important values that are the foundation of care for ourselves, and others.

We acknowledge our spiritual life to be the foundation of our family. We teach and cherish the principles of care and love for each other, the values of the golden rule, the human rights that guarantee freedom, the work that creates abundance, and the spirit of celebration that is a gratitude for the good we have and the good we can share with others.

Our home is a place of safety where each of us can express our needs, our pain, and our joy. It is a place where we can dare to be vulnerable and feel safe. It is a place where we will model cooperation, collaboration, and teamwork. We will honor the individual differences and talents of ourselves as adults and of our children, and model how we can share, learn, and work together.

The Kamatsu Family Mission Statement

We are committed to meet the basic needs of ourselves and our children.

We will teach and practice values that will enhance and enrich each of us as we do our work and as we, both adults and children, are leaders in our community.

We are committed to the education of our children, ensuring that they learn all they can from the schools they attend and can take the best of what they learn and put it into action.

We make our home a safe place where emotions can be expressed.

We take direct responsibility for teaching our children ethics, basic economics, and the values of competition and cooperation.

We honor, share, and teach what we have learned from our parents and grandparents through their life stories, their wisdom, and their spiritual guidance.

We will always remember, honor, and celebrate the lives of our ancestors, those related to us and those from our heritage and great cultural tradition.

The Sign of Laima
This symbol reminds us about joy, personified joy
that belongs to all of us. It is our destiny. It is about
the possibilities each of us have to celebrate, to
actually live the happiness and joy we find in our
lives and in each other. And yet with the promises
come the responsibility, the biggest of which is
to remember that both love and happiness
are also decisions.

As you create your marriage, may your creativity, persistence
and endurance always find itself in a relationship of joy.

Part 4

Dealing with Challenges
to Successful Marriage

The fourth part of this book is about giving leadership to your marriage. It is about being proactive in your relationship. Don't count on your love to keep your marriage alive. Count on your marriage to keep your love alive.

If you have followed the book as it is written, you have been on a remarkable journey to reach this point. The first part celebrated and chronicled your togetherness, romance, and the truths you hold dear in your relationship. The second part introduced you to the possibility of making decisions about the four biggest problem areas of marriage including communication, relatives and in-laws, money, and sexual intimacy. The third part explored commitment and making common decisions to fortify and support your relationship.

Part Four is essentially about giving leadership to your relationship and will deal with the deep sense of couple-connection, the problems that pull couples and marriages apart, and how to understand and deal with those forces.

Chapter 13

Love, Spirit, Health,
and the Sustainable Household

 I am creating my marriage
with creativity, persistence and endurance
always finding the possibility of joy.

Chapter 13

*A*n exciting if somewhat strange thing can happen to a relationship as it progresses. As couples learn to accept each other and accept that they do not have to change each other, they learn to give honor to their relationship just as it is. This understanding becomes a faith stance that moves couples past pettiness, inflexibility, silly complaints, and arguments.

Even as the two of you work to keep your marriage sound, an unforeseen and unplanned next step happens. The bond between you deepens. Perhaps for no reason you can put your finger on, each of you begins to see something new or different in the other. It is like catching a glimpse of the divine in your lover.

You begin to have a deeper appreciation for each other's gifts, which might include expressions of compassion, loving kindness, collaboration, and teamwork. You begin to experience a shift in your relationship. The realization of this phase may start out as a simple expression of gratitude that sounds something like this, "I'm sure lucky. I thank God I have _____ in my life."

This statement is not made in the midst of a perfect marriage. Each of you may know one another so well that you understand each other's faults very well. You may even begin to see that faults have their own kind of gift. The two of you honor each other and the way life is. You may also notice even in showing your partner a small consideration that you feel a deeper connection to all of life. In these moments, couples realize even without having the perfect marriage partner, that they truly have found in each other their soul mate.

Love, A Celebration of Life

Lovemaking also takes on a special sense of celebrating life. It is as if in the middle of sex, you experience being in touch with all that is. There can be a feeling you and Creation are merging. You realize as you make love to your lover that you are also worshiping. You often experience both a sense of elation and humility. You feel Spirit.

Spirit can also surface simply in the way you communicate. It pops up in the daily thank-yous and honest compliments you give each other. Spirit emerges strongly in the overall relationship mood as well. Spirit in marriage is nurtured when both partners understand the reasons for gratitude and express them.

A Couple's Journey to Maturity and Intimacy

Couples do not reach a state of intimacy and bliss with each other simply by wishing for it. It takes learning. It takes work. Here is a true story about this idea.

When I was letting other readers review the book, one of my volunteer editors recounted a story that illustrates, in a very practical way, the points here. She reflected on her marriage that lasted over half a century. This story illustrates how one couple began to move past the conflict and competition stage of marriage, to cooperation and later a deeper intimacy.

She and her husband, although they already had children, were still caught in a sense of quarreling. She was finally fed up with her husband and decided to get professional advice from a psychiatrist. Upon meeting the doctor she unburdened herself of her troubles and plaintively asked, "How can I change my husband?"

It took two meetings with this therapist for her to realize that, in fact, no one really changes the other person. After a long discussion on how she, not her husband, could change, the doctor wanted to know what the worst complaint was about her husband. She explained that every time her husband got a phone call, the whole family had to stop what it was doing so that he could talk. This seemed to be unfair since there was an extension phone that he could use instead.

After this session, a little later in the week, her husband got another phone call while the family was watching TV. He surprised his wife by saying, "Honey, I can get this call on the extension phone." After the call my friend stomped in to confront her husband. "You've been talking to my doctor, haven't you?" Her husband was flummoxed and completely taken aback by the comment. He truly had not spoken with the therapist but had decided to change this behavior on his own.

This was an eye-opening event. Her dialogue with her husband was truly, even though slowly, beginning to change. They still bickered but not in the way they had before. One day when her husband found that his wife had once again done something that displeased him, he demanded of her, "Why did you do that?"

Exasperated and not sure how to answer, since she had not meant any harm, she finally said the funny and incredible, "Well dear, when I awoke this morning I asked myself what could I do today to tick off my husband and this is what I came up with."

Their relationship was strong and both were able to laugh at this funny answer. Even with progress in the relationship, there still were some disagreements. One day her husband flat out said to her, "We're not planning to get a divorce, are we?" She agreed they did not intend to divorce. He said, "Well, why don't we act like it?"

This encounter finally changed from then on the whole nature of their future conversations. They remembered that they had decided to be each other's best friend. At this point the conflictive, competitive behavior of the power struggle completely stopped. Instead they entered into a cooperative, collaborative stage of marriage in which they really did act as if they were good friends.

The Negativity Trap

In this important discussion, it is crucial to learn that negativity does not have to dominate your marriage and that there are approaches to taking healthy attitudes and relationships to one another. It is also about how to reverse the negativity that couples can fall into.

Negativity can consume a marriage. Negativity is a creepy, strange monster that can invade our brains and our relationships. Negativity can lead to divorce and undermine goodwill, intimacy, and the possibility of reconciliation.

Even mature marriages can struggle with it. Reflection time is needed to grasp what negativity does in a marriage. As if watching a video, fast forward on the remote to the end. It is often when negativity has taken its toll and when marriage has failed that well-meaning friends want to search for the reasons "why." Your friends may not be directly accusatory but sometimes they ask intrusive questions. "What happened?" This question can sound like "What did you do wrong?" Another question that's more reflective and hopefully more positive may emerge: "What did you learn?"

There is no escaping this truth: you are responsible for the health of your relationship.

The Unforeseen Challenges

New challenges can and do intervene to upset the happy married life. Events can sabotage a marriage-overwhelming events that must be dealt with. Knowing that there are things beyond your control, the question becomes how do you sidestep the blame game and take a new, healthy, positive relationship to your marriage? Giving some thought in advance of a crisis is healthy. Being forewarned is being forearmed.

Here is a partial list of some overwhelming and some not-so-overwhelming situations couples deal with:

1. One of you suffers a catastrophic health crisis.

2. A mental illness occurs in which one or both of you need treatment.

3. Alcohol consumption becomes a crisis and gets worse over time.

4. Street or prescription drugs continue to be abused.

5. "Rogue" family members interfere in family harmony.

6. The media, movies, TV shows, and/or magazines make it appear your marriage is not okay.

7. There are advances from would-be lovers, for example, at work.

8. Physical weariness halts sexual intimacy.

9. Child rearing brings on physical exhaustion.

10. Career demands steal time from legitimate family activities.

11. Extended work time, over involvement in work, is used to avoid dealing with your marriage problems.

12. One or both of you lose jobs, straining your budget, and you must live with the stress of making do.

13. Feelings of personal vulnerability stop real communication.

14. One partner blames the other for their own interior challenges.

15. Shopping becomes an escape from your own marriage issues.

16. Your children play divide and conquer pitting you against each other.

17. Your spouse favors the children over you.

18. Your spouse favors their parents over you.

19. Both of you are thrown into grief at the death of a family member or even your child.

These are challenges that demand time for reflection, authentic and civil conversation, maturity, and leadership to resolve. What other negative influences or situations would you add to this list? What would you identify as sabotaging influences for your relationship?

Families in Crisis: An Emergency

There are probably some in the list above that sound familiar. Here is a warning. Do not take this situation lightly. These are not situations to be ignored; these are situations in which negativity can become dominant in your conversations. Negativity related to big challenges can lead to fighting and condemnation of one another.

If you are not able to talk these things out and still resolve that you are friends and lovers, you have come to a more dire situation. In this instance your relationship is experiencing an emergency!

You may not, at least not at first, recognize any one of these problems as a "make it or break it" situation. But problems and negativity can build. Take steps to get help. Fast. If, for example, the disagreements and the sense of condemnation is not turned around, it becomes the crucial factor that often eventually can lead you to divorce.

Most of us don't realize that we all have been trained to be competitive. As an example, it is not uncommon to get heated watching sports and even show disdain for the players. Marriage, however, is not a football game; it is not a way to make the basket over your partner's defensive guarding and not a way to run the bases and score. These ideas are all around us. Most of our education and sports exposure teaches us about competition. As a society we are not used to thinking about our relationships in a win-win way.

Generally speaking, there is a belief that in every relationship outcome someone must win and someone must lose. In marriage, if your idea wins you might assume your partner thinks you are right. However that may not be the case. Your partner may think it is not worth the fight. This, you see, is still a win-lose situation.

If you are a naturally competitive person-as mentioned before, we are all on some level taught to be-are you conscious of it? This often can be a negativity that is dangerous. To make peace in the marriage usually one of the partners is left to resentfully say, "I lost on this but, you know what, I can't always win. I will win another day." So the win-lose framework of negativity thinking keeps on going.

Expressions of negativity can directly attack the spiritual underpinnings of relationships. Negativity also can physically weaken the body, leave emotional wounds, and damage your marriage. Negativity then dominates the expressions within a marriage; negativity can become a self-perpetuating cycle.

A lot of negativity can show up as a partner's anger, inflexibility, or a sense of arrogance. The expression of arrogance often forms around the idea of: "I'm right and you're wrong!" Sometimes the next expressions can go to a more dangerous communication: that of condemnation or disdain for your partner.

Communication, reflection, and time can heal these situations. There are those times when each of you may want to do your "work." Who, for goodness' sake, as an individual or as a couple wants to deal with their baggage, shame, guilt, or other failures all the time? However, if there is not good progress between the two of you in terms of examining and dealing with your lives, and if disdainful attitudes continue in your marriage, you most likely will lose your relationship. If you are serious about your life together, then marriage counseling is a positive alternative. And as always is better for couples if they can access help early rather than later.

Marriage and Faith Traditions

Questions of faith in your marriage may require your attention. There is nothing about formally joining a faith that necessarily guarantees a successful marriage. Often couples marry outside of their own religions. Some of you may marry without having strong ties to faith. You may have decided to be on your own journey without formal involvement in a religion. Some of you may say you are "spiritual but not religious."

However belonging to a faith has helped marriages. Many couples, in seeking and finding a tradition to belong to, have also found they have a closer connection to each other and to community. If your religion makes sense to you, you can also derive both personal satisfaction and a mission direction from actively participating in it. It may, if you have children, provide them a way to learn basic ethics and how to maintain healthy relationships.

Perhaps you have noted that all of us as human beings orient ourselves to seek and express spirit? It appears that within our genetic blueprint, all of us tend to come wired, one way or another, to be spiritual or, as some people call it, religious. Our programming does not tell us to belong to a specific religion; it simply shows up as our spiritual consciousness. All of us seek the solace of faith, yearn to be connected to all that is, and express ultimate concerns about life.

When and if you do have children, it will be your responsibility to teach them to be fair, kind, discerning, accountable, forgiving, and compassionate. Sometimes belonging to a religion can help us teach those important values. We also know faith teachings in our earliest childhood years-such as learning the golden rule, what is basically right and wrong, and to respect differences in other people-are critical in forming who we are, how we act, and who we become.

As we have said before, there is a lot the two of you can do to give leadership to your relationship. This section has been written so the two of you can explore your ideas and agreements about attitudes, relationships, spirit, and health.

Since your spiritual and religious views have so much to do with the success of your marriage, we will explore them in the questions below. Spirit, health, and sexuality have greater dimension than is covered here. Please add to your thinking with the following starter questions. It is important!

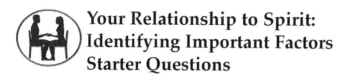

Your Relationship to Spirit: Identifying Important Factors Starter Questions

It is a pretty good assumption that the two of you have had a lot of discussion about sex. So the starter questions start at a higher level of thinking. As always these are starter questions and feel free to include and answer your own questions.

1. Do both of you come from the same religious tradition? What are the best things about your tradition?

2. If you are from different backgrounds, how important are the differences? Is there room for understanding and compromise?

3. How do you view traditional holidays and what holidays do you celebrate?

4. What kinds of celebrations do you think will be important for your family?

5. Have each of you talked about your understanding of spirit and your connections to formal religion?

6. What is it in your faith experience that your partner needs to understand, so the two of you can make a better decision about belonging to a formal religion? What will your approach be?

7. Do the two of you feel the need to belong to a formal religion, or is it something you can put off, at least for now?

8. What if you have children? Will you raise them in a faith tradition?

9. What about your own wedding? Will it take place in a church, synagogue, mosque, or temple?

10. How do you see the role of spirit in your own lives? What role do you hope spirit will play in your marriage?

11. What illustrates how faith has strengthened your friendship?

12. Have you caught glimpses of how you might be soul mates? What are those?

13. How have you already given leadership to your relationship? What did you do?

Chapter 14

Anger, Cheating, and Divorce:
Being Forewarned Is Being Forearmed

 I am creating my marriage
with creativity, persistence and endurance
always finding the possibility of joy.

Chapter 14

*I*n this chapter we are dealing with anger because when it is abused, misunderstood, or denied, it often becomes the underlying cause in destroying intimacy and the one factor that eventually leads to divorce.

Not everyone is taught about anger when growing up. Many young couples, to their surprise, find that they do not know how to deal with their anger or the anger of their partner. Many couples somehow stay married for years and never learn to effectively deal with anger.

Many people do not relate well to the whole range of emotions including anger, joy, sadness, fear, and shame. How the two of you understand emotions and how you relate to them plays a large part in how successful your marriage will be. It takes emotional intelligence to make a marriage work. This is especially true for anger.

Many people do not know where anger comes from or how it operates. It is sometimes called a "stealth emotion" since it seems to sneak up on people. Anger, although it can be a healthy emotion, is usually thought of as the "big problem".

Identifying, understanding, and naming your own emotions, especially anger, is a critical part in giving your marriage the maturity and therefore leadership it requires. It may seem strange that so much emphasis is given to emotions and anger in this chapter. However, anger's impact usually plays a role in practically every marriage crisis.

In our society there is a "common sense" saying that men show anger easily but have trouble dealing with sadness. For women the reverse is true. Women easily embrace sadness but deny or flee from anger. However, what is very common is that both men and women can deny being angry even after just having displayed anger. It is true that both of you either are or have been angry, probably very angry. When anger goes unrecognized and disrespected, it can come out as sabotaging behaviors or show up as illness.

Once, in my therapy role, I was running an anger management group. In it were reluctant people who did not believe they had an anger issue, but who had come to it because of pressure from others. They were what I call the "anger deniers." One woman insisted that she never got angry but admitted to frustration, upset, and disgust. All of these might be called anger but she had been taught that anger was wrong. What is interesting with many in these groups was that even after my efforts to explain how anger emerges, how it serves as a defense when boundaries are crossed, and how it cannot be ignored, many still claimed they were never angry.

What I hope you will realize is that denied anger can take a devastating toll. Often it slips out sideways in snide remarks and destructive behaviors and can even be played off as being cute or just some passing little trick. Anger deniers are often passive-aggressive and when they hurt others they can pretend that, of course, it was never intentional. The worst of the deniers often say, "I don't get angry. I just get even." The worst of these do dastardly acts like poison, drown, push off a cliff, or smother their sleeping spouses. Of course, they claim they don't get angry but their rage goes unchecked.

Here are some other critically important ideas about anger. What you learn here may be exactly what it may take to have a happy marriage. It is important to know and understand healthy anger and how it differs from unhealthy anger. They are not the same. As I explain this emotion, I ask you to be aware of the difference between anger and rage. It is very important to distinguish between them. However, it is a fact that rage does show up when daily angers are ignored and disrespected for too long.

Expressions of anger, especially those coming from your lover, are, surprisingly enough, usually words of caring. You may not like the words but often they are based on real concern and love. It is not a time to strike back with an attack to show your partner "what for." If you can, take a breath and make the effort to listen.

Again take a deep breath. Your lover, your best friend, may be upset but, in almost every case, it is not the huge crisis it might seem at the moment. The anger emotion is not usually a deal-breaking upset that leads to indifference or an end to your relationship.

Usually anger expressed directly, cleanly, and to the point will lead to understanding and even to what we call a "fair fight." It is always better to express anger but it is also important how it gets said. Though in the heat of a moment it may not be possible, it is, of course, a somewhat better situation that anger and all of the emotions are expressed with thought-out "I-statements."

After your argument, when done well or at least well enough, you will find that the air is cleared and believe it or not, you still will love each other just as deeply-if not even more.

Sometimes, not often, anger emerges suddenly in response to an immediate danger or insult. However, earlier I said that anger is a stealth emotion. Most anger is sneaky. In my experience, many people deny being angry. It is not that they are lying. It is more likely they don't understand how anger works.

It is more typical for people to say, "I just feel hurt. I'm not angry." However, as the hurt is experienced, without your conscious permission, anger, the partner of hurt, emerges. People are usually so conscious of whatever other emotional pain they experience that they miss the anger that has arisen.

Some people tend to express anger easily. Too many turn it inwards. For some the simple statement, "I have a problem with that" is too fearful and can seem like confrontation. Too many people elect to just shut up instead of expressing the simplest statements of anger. Even if their anger is proportional to the experienced problem, they stuff and elect to be unhappy rather than to be unburdened.

Anger, along with its partners fear and anxiety, often creates the basis for depression. Most of us therapists believe that depression is the number one illness in the world. It has possibilities of being such a destructive mood state that it can sink families and marriages. While depression has many sources, it is also true that an angry person will not reverse depression without dealing with their own anger.

There is one more critical thing to understand about anger. We have already talked about anger as it relates to depression. The unhealthy anger-the one that does not see the light of day, that is repressed and held inside-transforms over time into a completely different or intensified emotional state called rage. The act of denying anger, and when in rage, there are so many ways to hurt your relationship, devastate your partner emotionally, and leave yourself feeling emotionally bankrupt and empty.

Healthy Anger Is Liberating

The healthy anger, which we have described above, clearly can work for the betterment of your relationship. Because it is usually based on caring and love, it eventually can build a stronger relationship. Expressing it authentically is what clears the air and let's you reconnect. However, rage is quite different.

Rage is destructive. Rage, unleashed in a flash, can even kill. Rage is born of stuffing down anger, ignoring its constructive benefits, and usually letting it fester for long periods of time.

Some of you, especially romantics-a hugely admirable quality-may think that this introduction to anger does not pertain to you and your love life. However, since anger is a sneaky emotion, it can block you from loving and being loved.

Stop and think about your history. Did your parents teach you to respect and honor anger? Perhaps you were told as a child that you should be seen and not heard. Did parents, teachers, or other adults make you feel guilty or ashamed for being angry? A typical statement from parents might be, "How dare you be angry? We slave everyday to put food on the table. You are an angry ingrate." Does any of this sound familiar?

You may also have been taught that anger is a wasted emotion. This idea has the implication that if you had the right thoughts, your anger would not be present. Some religious or spiritual advisors share this point of view. There is some limited truth to this idea. For saints, for a person of advanced "love consciousness," anger is a completely different proposition. That may be also the difference between YOU and, say, someone like Mother Teresa. Since most of us are not saints, it is a good idea to respect anger and to learn to use it well. Perhaps that is even the saints' secret.

When you thoroughly know that the causes of a particular anger are no longer important, anger all on its own, takes its leave. It disappears. This can also happen as you learn to forgive. When you know in your mind and, so to speak, in your heart, that you no longer need the burden of a particular anger, that anger disappears. It disappears all by itself. There is more good news. Unhealthy anger, the kind closely related to rage, can usually be successfully reversed when you learn to express anger in healthy ways. If this is too difficult, then you can learn to deal with it by getting professional help.

The two of you lovers, no doubt, have had a chance to share secrets and say things you would not tell anyone else. It is wonderful to unburden, to share and trust. What a great way to release anger! As courtship gets serious, it is common for couples to share many hurts and tribulations. Anger may have been present. You both may have dealt with it well. It is then you can feel a mutual trust. A commonly expressed sentiment is, "At last I've found somebody who listens, who loves me, and really cares who I am."

Truth, speaking your own truth, must flourish along with friendship and love. After all, if you have friends who cannot accept the real you, are they really your friends? Do they really love you? If you always have to pretend you are sweet and never angry, is that the real you? Being the real you matters. Your marriage could be stifled and cut off from intimacy by the pretense because you decide not to deal with your real emotions.

Cheating and Consequences

Now that we have discussed anger and its implications, you may also see that anger plays a role in cheating. Cheating rarely happens without anger. If you have read and answered the Starter Questions in Part III, you have some strong ideas of what you want in marriage. You also have some intellectual understanding of what cheating is for you.

What actually happens when a partner cheats? How does it happen that so many angry situations stay unresolved? Where does love go when love goes away? Couples are often confused and these questions can seem more profound after a marriage-threatening crisis. In the midst of anger, love dwindles away; little bit by little bit, it can slowly disappear.

Fights, for example, dealing with money issues, or a health crisis are often too consuming to allow many couples to look at the bigger picture. Hopefully in the bigger picture you can see that you love each other in spite of going through a rough patch. If fights are not resolved, one or the other of you may begin to think that "the grass is greener on the other side of the fence."

With the practice of denying and stuffing anger, some couples come to the point where one or both will say to themselves, "He (she) does not care about me, so I do not care about her (him)." For some, cheating becomes an easy alternative.

Several times in this book there were recommendations to get counseling or therapy. When fights cannot be easily resolved, it is a very strong indicator that it is time to get professional help. It is never too late to get therapy. However, the earlier therapy is introduced into the situation the more that can be done to heal breaches and restore or rebuild a relationship.

Often continuous fighting reflects inexperience and immaturity. Looking for love elsewhere rather than resolving your relationship issues also reflects immaturity. Seeking love elsewhere-as the country song says, "looking for love in all the wrong places"-often acts to transfer your hurt, confusion, and interior baggage to the new, other person, while you are wasting time by not dealing with the relationship you have. And of course, cheating on your relationship also means cheating on yourself.

Of course, if you know absolutely that your marriage is over, it is so much better to make a clean break. A clean break, dealing first with what is broken, is better than attempting to make a new and better deal with a new lover while you are in the old relationship. If your marriage is over, then it is really over. Otherwise, I encourage you to have the courage to work through your differences.

What people often say and what people do are often two different things. It is rare that a partner is clueless that their relationship is faltering. What may be closer to reality is that people bring denial into their marriage, and they may want to hide from painful truths. Couples in crisis may have even learned previously many harmful ways of acting and thinking. One of them may be a self-imposed censor regarding what can be said and what can't be said to your partner. However, not communicating may be the death of your relationship.

Many things are involved if your situation has taken a turn such that one of you is having an affair. Usually if one partner is having an affair, the affair in and of itself is not the most significant problem. Affairs are a problem. However, usually there are unresolved issues present in the marriage, even before the affair gets started.

Sometimes when one or the other cheats, it is because the marriage relationship is unfulfilling, or it feels unfulfilling. Two things can be involved. One is that the unhappy partner has not learned to ask for what he or she needs. The second is that for many couples there is a common illusion: my partner must make me happy and happiness must come from outside of me.

Both of these scenarios indicate that the unhappy partner has personal work to do. When the unhappy partner moves into an affair, he or she is also cheating on himself or herself. There are emotional consequences for both partners.

However, people with serious mental issues or people that we commonly call sexually addicted may have extramarital affairs whether things are going well in the marriage or not. Or, on the other hand, things are never getting better in the marriage because of one partner's serious issues. Unfortunately many people with these serious conditions usually do not make good marriage partners. Some people simply should not get married.

Talking out misunderstandings and expressing needs and wants is the first option. What can make a difference is to confront the problems early, in order to create helpful change, perhaps using "I statements" introduced early or, if necessary, going to therapy.

Loving couples most often can make adjustments when communication is a challenge and by sticking with it they can resolve these situations. When engaged in the struggle, some use a rule that says that neither couple can leave the "ring." In other words they decide not to leave the discussion just because they are unhappy, or it feels uncomfortable.

However, if companionship and sexual needs continue not to be met, the therapy option is better than divorce. In cases like these, both of you are strongly encouraged to try therapy early before your relationship becomes more problematic.

In this book, we have emphasized questions designed to make you think, to dig for answers and look at your own feelings and motivations. This kind of reflection is called doing your own work. For your marriage to be successful, this work is expected to continue through the years to come. It is the way life is. Doing your own work about what is going on with you is not only a way to honor yourself, but can allow you to see your partner in a different light as well.

Interestingly, very often, the partner who cheats has stopped doing this kind of personal work. Of course, sometimes in cases where communication is frozen, when a partner does his or her work and the work is not acknowledged or accepted by the other spouse, the partner feels frustrated and hopeless, and so decides to cheat out of anger and revenge.

Here is the part about cheating that is not often said. So here we say it again: sadly, cheating on your partner is also cheating on yourself.

Cheating and Addiction

Often therapists have a viewpoint that many couples ordinarily do not. Many therapists see addiction as cheating, since alcohol and drugs can act as and simulate being a partner in the marriage relationship. Here are some of the problems of addiction and also a kind of cheating that is related to it.

Cheating does not always manifest itself in an affair with another person. Quitting or stopping the normal flow of conversation, deciding to quit communication, and deciding not to be present to the relationship could also be considered cheating. Therapists recognize that cheating can take place outside, as well as inside, a marriage.

For example, there are relationships to chemical substances that can easily be considered as forms of cheating. Addictions to alcohol or to a street drug, or even a prescribed drug when abused, can substantially change relationships. Often the addictive substance is so dominant that in and of itself, it becomes the significant other. For example, booze or cocaine is the lover. It is not an overstatement to say alcohol and drugs can act as a lover or be the lover.

The sober partner knows there is something very wrong, but may not give the name "cheating" to the partner's dependence or addiction. The sober one may even be trapped into enabling the abusive patterns of the intoxicated partner. Alcohol, for example, is often a very demanding lover. Alcoholics often would rather die than not get their fix. The alcoholic's loyalty to their chemical can be nearly unshakable. It is a love affair, and this type of drinking is by most definitions very serious and can be considered the same as cheating.

Anger, not dealt with, long held anger is usually also a major factor in alcoholic behavior. While genetic predisposition is present for most alcoholics, hurt, anger, and fear can reinforce addiction. Emotional patterns from early childhood experiences can and do shape alcoholism and drug abuse.

There are couples that have mutually engaged in long-term, regular drinking whose marriages have not ended in divorce. In outward appearances many of these couples can make adjustments to appear as normal, cordial people. Whether they can or should be called drunks or addicted is not the issue here. On the inside, what is happening is that the progressive power of alcohol keeps attacking every organ of the body.

Drinking couples often forgo a wide range of intimacy experiences and substitute instead the jovial high from alcohol. After years of steady drinking, this couple's true bond becomes keeping one another drunk. This reflects their agreement, a type of mutuality, in which because of their drinking they are often the most important people to each other. This can be a very tiring way to live.

Whether one or both are drinking, both begin to create and interact in a hierarchy based on their substance use. In the case of a sole drunken partner, he or she pushes away the sober partner and imposes on that partner the job of being a codependent servant. Other people are moved ahead as being more important than the sober spouse. This is especially true if the sober partner is not an enabler. These other people include those who buy drinks and people who drink with the alcoholic partner. On the ladder of important people, almost any drunk can be more important than the sober spouse and that spouse can easily be relegated-and this is not unusual-to, say, the eighth or even the tenth place down in the relationship ladder.

Dealing with Anger and Problem Solving Starter Questions

1. This is a good place to assess your communication abilities. For example, what have the two of you learned about fighting fairly?

2. Can you resolve your differences without dragging them out for days? If not, how might you practice fighting fairly?

3. Here are three questions to consider together: Are the two of you able to express your innermost feelings and fears? Do you feel safe doing so? What might you do to create an increased sense of safety for the two of you?

4. Do you find yourself afraid to see your partner vulnerable? If you fear vulnerability, how might you discuss dealing with these fears? What reassurance do you need?

5. Do you acknowledge and give credit to your partner's positive efforts on a daily basis? Even if mutual goals are not yet fully achieved, do you give credit where it is due?

6. Do you give honest compliments? If not, do you understand what keeps you from doing so? How might you honor your partner's efforts

7. If you cannot verbally express gratitude, are there other ways you express thanks?

8. Do any of these show up in your relationship: unresolved resentments, continued fault finding, and feelings of condemnation? These are strong indicators that your journey together will end in divorce. What are you willing to do to reverse these negative emotions to save your marriage?

9. What has been your experience with alcoholics and drug abusers?

10. Have you or your partner had a time in your life when drinking or drug use were out of control? Perhaps you participated in this activity in your school days. How have you handled it?

11. Consider if this applies to you. If you are drinking or using drugs, are you willing to relinquish your relationship as a couple to a chemical substance?

12. Because drugs and alcohol diminish sexuality, are you willing to give up your potential for a good sex life to these chemicals?

13. If substance abuse is a problem, how might you discuss this situation with each other? Are you, both of you, willing to get help? What action are you both willing to take to change?

Chapter 15

The Challenges of Family Crisis

 I am creating my marriage
with creativity, persistence and endurance
always finding the possibility of joy.

Chapter 15

*C*rises happen. People get sick. People lose jobs. There are accidents. People's spirits can crash. These things can and will challenge your relationship.

You may have happily and successfully steered your relationship through the stage of romance. Even though the romance has faded a bit, you are still very much in love. With luck and your enlightened participation, you have gotten past the stage of marriage that is marked by conflict and competition. This latter stage often begins when the romance stage ends. Besides the crisis-causing situations we listed earlier, there is one ongoing reason couples are in conflict. It is competition. It is the need to win, sometimes phrased as the need to be right.

It is the underlying cause of conflict through which many relationships do not and cannot survive. This is so pronounced in marriages that it is considered a "stage" of marriage. It is a stage when disagreements and conflicts materialize and continue. This is the energy which eventually leads to divorce. The number one reason for divorce, the number one reason, is that one or both you would rather win than cooperate and build a relationship. You may not believe this, especially as you are just starting out, but fighting, competing, and attempting to win can dominate a relationship.

The stage of marriage that is marked by the most intimacy is one in which there is collaboration and cooperation. Couples relate to each other well in problem-solving and work together for the sake of creativity and generativity. This is a stage in which physical intimacy and intellectual compatibility can be, and often is, strongly enhanced.

The magic of having a partner is that in times of crisis you are not alone. Hopefully, your partner has become your best friend. You and your best friend are going through this crisis, whatever it may be, together. Perhaps you may find yourself very appreciative since your best friend, your wife or husband, is supporting you as you go through a crisis. You know you are not alone.

Your companionship is even more magical because you have the power to say the words your partner needs to hear. In loving your partner you can experience a certain dimension: when you undertake to give love and support you may realize that not only you are giving strength to your partner but also giving strength to yourself. Somehow in these cases the more you love, the more courage you have.

In being there in the relationship, in being able to be supportive, each of you must move past the blame game. Each of you needs to be aware of your own internal baggage. You each have burdens that are specifically yours. Your partner can be there beside you but cannot take your burdens away from you. Each of you is on an individual journey. Each of you is on a journey alone but together. Best friends. Hopefully together.

And there is more. You will be challenged more since both of you will continue to change as people. The question is how each of you can support the individual and joint aspects of this journey--your journey as a couple. How do individual changes complement your relationship? How can you continue to lend strength to each other?

So look around you. Are there couples around who support each other as they are undergoing change? How do they handle change? Find people who have come through to the other side of a health crisis. From what you learn from these special couples, imagine what you might do with the challenges or a crisis in your life. What makes the difference in getting through a crisis? What does spirit have to do with it?

Here are some questions to help you discover approaches that can build your partnership. Most couples (and this may include you) about to marry have not experienced life-shaking crisis or major health threats. However, if you have been in these situations, reflect on what you learned and how people helped you through your challenges. Fortunately, all of the possible things that might go wrong do not usually all happen at one time.

Talking about Leadership in Times of Crisis Starter Questions

1. Do you know couples that have made it through hard times? If so, how do they talk about the adversity of making it through their tribulation?

2. Perhaps in your relationship the two of you have had to deal with difficult situations. If so, how did you handle it? How do people salvage something from destructive experiences?

3. Do you communicate well with one another? How do you think partners can provide support and avoid judgment when the other shares something very personal?

4. Closer to home, have you seen your parents or other family members deal with tough situations? What was your experience of what happened? What did you learn?

5. At what point have you given each other support in a time of crisis?

6. What health practices have you noticed that couples are undertaking either to prevent problems or after they have gone through their problems?

7. What do all of those things you have talked about tell you about leadership?

Divorce

There was a time in the United States, as well as many places in the world, when divorce was talked about in amazement and wonder. It was a rare happening which was instigated by unusual events or involved a few celebrities like movie stars or the very rich. Up until the second half of the last century, the reasons accepted as common sense for getting a divorce included reasons of incompatibility as follows:

1. A partner was caught cheating.

2. One of the partners was addicted to alcohol and or drugs.

3. One of the partners was intentionally physically violent to the other.

4. One of the partners was mentally ill. (Remember this was a time when either there was no medication or the medication available did not work well).

It is somewhat surprising now that many relationships end for different reasons than the ones above. They can sound like, "We just outgrew each other" or "We fell out of love" or "We were both too young and immature when we married."

There is another dynamic that is a part of the divorce picture. This has to do with couples that are a part of a rescue. A rescue scenario gets established when an eager potential mate learns he or she can help a potential newfound lover out of some dire emergency. For example, this can include financial assistance in paying off overwhelming bills for the new lover. The resulting interaction between the couples creates an illusion that the couple is compatible; they are "meant to be."

Some of these relationships actually work out. It is obvious the rescue dynamic has taken place millions of times and divorce has not always been the result. In fact, there are many happy marriages that started with a rescue, usually by the man rescuing the woman or, nowadays, the woman rescuing a man. So why is rescue getting attention and being linked to divorce?

The problem with marrying the rescued person is the rescued person often grows to be dissatisfied with the partner and needs to be rescued again. That is to say, the rescued person becomes angry and disillusioned that their rescuer/lover is not doing enough for them. The rescued person often decides to cheat and seek out a new lover. The causes of why the original rescue was necessary are often never dealt with. What underlies this situation is the rescued significant other either cannot or does not step into an actual partner role. Immaturity is certainly involved. Either this person is incapable of commitment and work, or perhaps simply may find it easier to stay a victim. Typically, it is then the rescued party begins to seek out another rescuer.

Other Causes of Divorce

Many other things can contribute to divorce. However, the biggest personal reason couples divorce is that one or both are more interested in winning and competition then they are in building their marriage. Being "right" and "showing your partner what's what" lead to more fighting and simply continue the ongoing power struggle. Many couples have not made adjustments to the fact that their interests overlap and so they can waste precious time in power struggles. Of course the ideal is to discover that cooperation works better.

However, there is one more, one big, often unspoken, cause of divorce. It is sociological. Many of us live in places where we are on speaking terms with our neighbors but we really don't know them and they do not know us. In our time, dysfunctional family and community usually underlies, one way or another, all of the other causes of marital unhappiness. The places we live and the ways we live have changed dramatically from the last century, especially since World War II. Much of the outside-of-marriage support, whether it is from family, neighbors, or even the town as a whole, is usually missing these days. Support of many types is always necessary for marriages to make it.

Family therapists who say a couple is three people have a good point. There is you, the couple, and then there is the two of you and then at least one other person who sees you as a unit, talks to you as if you are family, and through action consciously or unconsciously, holds you in your marriage with all its problems and possibilities. This person is a mirror who gives a reinforcing positive reflection. This support role is often missing as we participate in bigger, faster, more urban and suburban life with huge economic pressures. An old sense of community has died (and is too often not re-created) and so too often has the sociological support that once was a part of past marriages.

It Takes Work to Make a Marriage

What are the factors that work against divorce but do not have to inevitably sink it? Keeping marriage together can sometimes seem hopeless. Doesn't the divorce rate spike toward sixty percent? Doesn't the advent of birth control mean having extramarital sex is easier? Isn't it possible that marriages get blown out of the water because of money, since our economy has changed and both partners have to work? No one is available for homemaking. The possibility of finding a lover on the job is always tempting.

There is only one thing that insures that a marriage will work. That one thing is the good will and dedicated personal efforts of both spouses. There are many, many reasons to make a marriage work. Marriage often supports emotional and physical health. Another reason is the very real high cost of divorce. The majority of families that function reasonably well will, in the long run, have a better standard of living and a better quality of life. Quality of life is very important, which also, in fact, has to do with your attitude. Quality of life is important by itself and is not the same as a higher standard of living.

There is a lot of quality that money can buy and a lot of quality it cannot. Quality of life includes a good working partnership, and emotional and physical happiness, having the richness of friendship. Quality of life can come from enjoying neighbors, family, friends, nature, faith, as well as enjoying a multitude of life activities including music, art, dance, and other creative endeavors. When this kind of quality is present, marriages can thrive.

Divorce is Not Cheap

Everyone in a divorce encounters a cost and pays a price. Divorce as a way of ending abuse is often necessary. This type of divorce can be a good thing. If the marriage is really over, divorce can create relief and freedom.

However, often divorce is devastating emotionally and psychologically. It is often interpreted as a failure. It means that the emotional bonds of marriage that for many support personal growth and undergird health are now cut. The partner that was supposed to be the best friend is no longer a best friend and often not a friend at all. Sometimes each partner experiences depression.

Children suffer as well. Sometimes they believe they are the cause of the breakup. While children can exasperate the marriage, they are not the adults or considered the responsible party in adult troubles. But kids don't always know that. Also, children often suffer financially because of the breakup. Sometimes the family home must be sold to resolve the dispute.

In society, there is a very small safety net for many people who become divorced, unemployed, or very ill. The divorced couple usually no longer supports one another in times of trouble. Whatever money or support that comes out of a divorce may, given the turmoil divorce can cause, impoverish both and does not make up for the emotional loss.

With all the burdens people face, family is the safety net most of us rely on. There may not be another way to take care of things. When divorce happens, the solution of keeping children with one parent is often not a good answer. It is possible that both partners, while collaborating together, could have more income and well-being, but with divorce are now forced to "make do" in more dire circumstances.

Often both partners have more stress and more illnesses. Sometimes the children go to the father, in which case the kids often terribly miss the mother. When the kids go to the mother, girls miss their father and boys often turn out to be big casualties of divorce. It is not so unusual that girls become rebellious and act out. Raised without a father, boys often will do badly in school, sometimes get into drugs and alcohol, or find their way into street gangs. Girls can lose a sense of direction and express a deeply felt father need.

Of course the cost for each family is different. Yet the cost is always there in some form.

Mental Challenges in Marriage

There are some problems that seem too big to handle. Many of them arise out of your decision-making and lifestyle.

Other challenges can come from health issues including mental health. Knowing what the mental challenges are to marriage is a big step in dealing with them, and creating a healthy lifestyle and a healthy marriage. After all, at one time or another many family members will need to deal with things like depression, stress, anxiety, and the need to make new adjustments.

Dealing successfully with mental challenges depends on perspective. It is important to remember no one escapes life without problems. Both partners have baggage. This perspective is one that says, "It's not just my partner. I have problems too." It is a perspective that can help with every-day problems and can help couples deal with mental issues.

Most of the challenges we face have stress in common. Stress is the number one illness symptom. Stress is also related to depression. Depression, not all of it by any means clinical, is the most common disorder or illness. Stress and depression help create a state of discomfort, dis-ease, frustration, and anger. They are major factors in heart and brain illnesses and disorders. They are a factor in debilitating the immune system and even in enabling cancer. What is important for you to know is that these states, stress and depression, can and do adversely affect your marriage.

Some of the problems that you bring to your marriage have their origin in your childhood. Most of us did not always get what we needed from our parents. Some of us almost never got what we needed. Parents are never perfect. All parents wound their children in some way. Stress, depression, our interior baggage is what we bring to marriage and the result often leads to misunderstandings.

You as a child did not have a vast life experience to help with reflection and understanding, so you were left to invent strategies to take care of yourself. As you grow and experience life, these strategies become less helpful. But all of us, in fact, rely on these strategies whether they are currently useful or not. The strategies often turn into burdens and the burdens are a large part of the interior baggage everyone brings into marriage.

One of the things we taught earlier in this book was how to approach, yes, care for, one another in tough times. We taught various approaches to communication. When dealing with stress, depression, frustration, and anger, it can be very easy to exchange hot words and bad thoughts. You have a choice in how you approach the other. You can avoid absolute statements, accusations, blame, and you can listen. You can take time to let your angry impulses settle. And most of all you can learn not to step into your partner's vulnerability, so to speak, avoiding adding insult to injury.

No one communicates perfectly. You will need practice. Those of us counselors and therapists who are supposed to be good at this also need practice. We, the experts, are not perfect communicators.

There are times when working on a specific problem is the only way that any progress can happen. This can lead to an effort to get clarity for your relationship, and even to begin healing your relationship. It is in this situation that a third party like a psychotherapist can often help. Usually as therapists we focus on the relationship and call it the object of therapy. It is one way of helping you work on your life together. Healing the relationship is the goal of couples therapy. Sometimes finding a healing path for each partner is also a necessary goal.

Your interior baggage created by childhood issues or the response to a crisis is something that you also bring into your marriage. These things can significantly weigh down your marriage. However, your marriage can survive these kinds of issues. There are also times when sadness and grief are appropriate and a necessary response to life experiences. In those times it can be reassuring to know you can turn to each other. You can derive solace from your relationship.

When There Are Specific Mental Issues

The reason for this section is that there are some mental illnesses that can end marriages. Many of you will still love one another, hope for the best with one another, and yet get divorced. Both of you may regret these circumstances.

The good news is that many of these challenges do not need to end your marriage. If you find yourself in this situation, for example, it may be that your partner is, in the larger view, pleased to have you and love you. It actually may not take a lot to make your marriage stronger, but there are times it will take the help of a professional.

Here we will discuss five very common mental challenges which often go undiagnosed and which when ignored can lead to divorce. They are depression, bipolar disorder, obsessive compulsive disorder, attention deficit hyperactivity disorder, and emotional and mental states related to substance abuse. You may not recognize many of these as being present or being a problem. However, even the sophisticated among us, even those who have graduate degrees, do not often understand mental challenges or illnesses.

It is good to know when to go for help. Dealing with the larger mental issues is one of those times. Getting the help you need can change the course of your life and even save a marriage, perhaps yours. You can know it is time to get help when people around you strongly suggest it and you find you cannot handle everyday tasks that you would expect to handle.

Here is something else. If your family is not directly affected by a mental illness, in close proximity-in your larger extended family, at the job, or in your community-someone you know has a mental illness. As said earlier, most people are unaware of someone else's illness.

We mentioned depression earlier. Depression can be sneaky. It is not always obvious. Some people suffer from depression and are unaware they have it. It may be, and is by many of us, considered the number one illness in the world. There are levels of depression from mild to serious. What most people refer to as mild depression is something that often can be handled without therapy and often fades away with time.

However, when a serious clinical depression does occur, it is time to get help. With either seemingly mild depression that does not go away or one with a sense of helplessness and overwhelming sadness, the best approach is to utilize the services of a therapist. Depression can kill. One out of five people die when suffering a major clinical depression.

Most of you as individuals and most of you as couples are not equipped to deal with resolving these more difficult issues. Neither are your friends and family. Friends and family sometimes are supportive, but they do not usually understand the illness or treatment.

Even if you have an economic hardship and cannot pay for counseling and therapy, it can be greatly beneficial to get professional help. And help is usually available in every area of the country. These services can be provided for through health insurance and Medicaid insurance. Otherwise you can often get it at steep discounts. Another source of help can be your family doctor.

So, focusing on your immediate family, there are health issues that can wear you down and tear at your relationship. There is hope and they do not need to destroy your relationship. However, they need to be understood. Here is a discussion of a handful of issues that affect families and often need attention.

First, let's look at drugs and drinking briefly. In the case of substance abuse, often the saner, more sober partner is worn out from giving kind and loving attention to the abusing partner. They become weary of what is called enabling. Many spouses believe that if only they could give their abusing partner kind attention, if they could love them more, that it would be possible to "love" their drinking or drugging ways into sobriety. Usually this does not work. Only a different brand of love, called tough love, can begin to make a dent in this very dysfunctional behavior.

Again, many sophisticated college grads do not fully understand alcoholism or substance abuse, even when they are living with a substance abusing partner. Contrary to popular belief, very often the more kindness that you give your spouse, the more into drink or drugs he or she will become. If your marriage has hope and possibility, then giving leadership to your relationship may mean learning about tough love and helping your partner get help. Sadly, for some, when abuse or addiction are severe, facing this truth can mean your marriage is over.

A second common challenge that is not always diagnosed is bipolar disorder. This may pertain to your marriage (or someone fairly close to you or someone you know in your community or work). For these people the range of behavior can be enthusiastically high to down in the dumps low and/or have mood swings somewhere in between. This disorder is not a moral failing but an organic situation; it is thought that the origins of this disorder have to do with chemical imbalances. If this seems to be a problem, do not simply jump to conclusions but talk these things out with a professional. If it happens that your partner's behavior, for example, is notably dysfunctional and disruptive in your relationship, you likely are not equipped to deal with it. Your partner may need medical attention and therapy.

A third common and too often undiagnosed mental challenge is obsessive compulsivity. There are two types one of which is a personality disorder. In both cases anxiety and fear play a role. The term, obsessive-compulsive, refers to obsessive thoughts that don't easily go away, and include driven or compulsive behaviors associated with those thoughts.

Although perfectionism plays a role in both types of these behaviors, it is the personality disorder type in which perfectionism is very pronounced. People with this type are driven to review, change, and refine, almost continually, something they are doing. The person with this disorder may exhibit an overly high sense of right and wrong, often based on ideas not shared by others, and have a need to do things according to a certain pattern or procedure and then even change their minds about the pattern or procedure.

This behavior is sometimes so intense that the person with this type is often seen as continually changing his or her mind. It is a pattern. They often appear to be flip-flopping and soon people close to them can stop trusting them. Those with this type of disorder cannot often understand why their spouse or co-workers do not get them.

However, very often spouses who try to give their very perfectionist partner consideration and kindness enable even more irrational strange behavior. In this way these patterns are somewhat similar to the ones which occur with alcohol. This person, in this case, is often emboldened to attempt even more perfect behavior. In cases like these, you may still find your partner attractive and think your marriage is viable. You may be very right. However, you yourself cannot treat your partner. Leadership here means encouraging him or her to get professional help.

Finally, another common condition that can slip detection because people disregard its seriousness is Attention Deficit Hyperactivity Disorder, sometimes known by the informal shorthand of ADD. Almost everyone has heard of ADHD because of its prominence in the news. Surprisingly many people have relatives or they themselves have these symptoms. This is an ancient problem and not just some modern day "invention"; it is said to have been described even by the very first doctors including Hypocrites. Sometimes it is misdiagnosed and sometimes it is underdiagnosed.

Again, this is a disorder that can negatively affect marriage. There are two major types. One is the hyperactive type ("ants in the pants") and the other is the inattentive ("daydreamer") type. Children with this disorder sometimes out grow it. Adults with ADHD have had it from childhood.

One example of a very common attribute for people with ADHD is that math quickly becomes dull, so for these adults balancing a checkbook is often a strain. People with ADHD also often have trouble with "transitions." That is, they complain that they cannot easily shift from having finished an old job to starting a new job. Symptoms can vary and ADHD can show up with other accompanying traits. Often some struggle with getting over-focused, over-indulged, almost locked or chained into an activity, and it takes a lot to pull them away from their present task.

Another real complaint goes something like this, "Once I think of something and think through how I could do it, my mind thinks I have done it and shuts off this activity."

In fact, many people with ADHD can often see the big picture but not be able to work out all of the smaller details of an operation. People with ADHD also can be very good working with many different kinds of people and often are good lovers, loyal to the marriage and loyal to you, the spouse.

Getting help for ADHD can be very important. Here again your family doctor can be a first place to get advice. Here is what can help: changing diet to increase nutrition, getting more exercise, avoiding sweets (especially in the morning), and being sure that you have all the necessary vitamins and minerals "on board." Often talk therapy based on a solutions approach can be very helpful and finally, if it is necessary, a prescription drug from your doctor can make a huge difference.

As you can see with OCD and ADHD in particular, and for other mental conditions in general, having a workable marriage is not hopeless. There is much more that might be said about mental challenges. However, the above information illustrates that many of these situations are not only hopeful but very workable. However, getting help from a professional is so often important that this one action-getting into therapy-could make or break a marriage.

There are marriages that survive in spite of the presence of a mental illness. In fact, some people with mental illnesses can be dynamic, interesting, and loving partners. Losing this marriage can also mean losing involvement with a very charming, exciting, if challenging partner. There are, of course, some mental illnesses that preclude intimacy in a partnership.

Chapter 16

Leadership, Love, and Therapy:
Courage to Stand Up
and Take Marriage-Saving Action

I am creating my marriage
with creativity, persistence and endurance
always finding the possibility of joy.

Chapter 16

*Y*ou may be a newlywed couple who has never been married before. Or you may be a couple that knows the reality of divorce. The following is valuable information for both of you: When you have been badly hurt, offended by the words or deeds of your partner, and angry words have been spoken, a devastating feeling can make it seem like the marriage is over. It can take a lot of courage to change and decide to heal your marriage in the midst of a shattering disagreement. There are times when only patience can help work to resolve problems. After you have tried everything, waiting is still better than taking action in the heat of anger.

If you hit snags, find yourself in a fight, and cannot figure out what the next step is, the worst thing to do, from my point of view, is to throw yourself into the arms of another. Usually being disloyal to your principles, to your understanding of marriage, and to your loved one will only complicate problems.

Often one partner, acting in a positive way, can decide to make the difference and begin to pull a marriage together. For this partner, there can be a huge sacrifice, since often healing a marriage can require setting aside personal hurt in order to save the relationship and the family. It takes some wisdom, which often allows a hurt or wronged partner to be the one who helps reconcile a broken relationship.

One thought to consider is that your partner has been your best friend and you may not find another person with similar qualities. Yet another thought is the understanding that the children, if you have them, will suffer in a divorce. Another is that in spite of the sadness and anger, there is still at least a small spark of love. In the midst of slights or betrayal sometimes one partner, despite what has happened, can see qualities that are still attractive in the other. In these cases, usually with a lot of courage, the hurt or betrayed partner accepts and forgives the other spouse. It is difficult to forgive but not impossible. It is difficult to believe you will love each other again, but not impossible.

There are many options and approaches. Sometimes compromise is the answer. Sometimes working or doing something the two of you can agree on, a kind of common ground, helps clarify things you cannot otherwise figure out. If there is something left of the marriage, it takes the courage of a leader to go to therapy. Doing something that brings the two of you a victory may be more important than living in anger or confusion. Doing something that works for you may allow you to find another way, a third way, to approach a seemingly insurmountable challenge.

When one or both individuals in the couple continually express "the right thing" and this stance keeps further dialogue from happening, your marriage can be badly impaired. Usually, the idea of "doing the right things" can seem to be normal. But an extreme approach to doing "a right thing" can be perfectionism in disguise. You'll know this is the case after a period of time, often when your joint decisions fall apart. If that's the case, then getting help from a therapist, a professional third party, may be the only way to resolve ongoing issues.

With hurt feelings, often no one wants to heal the situation. For example, one action might be to declare a time of talking and forgiveness. Sometimes one of you has to step up and be a leader. It takes real guts to be willing to do uncomfortable things to keep your marriage going.

Sometimes wanting to keep a marriage going may be all that keeps a marriage going. But it may be enough for the two of you to come to common ground, find a new victory, and begin the dialogue that allows reconciliation. Sometimes in the turmoil surrounding illness, a death, or a lost job, you may forget what it is that makes you a couple. You may have lost that "loving feeling" and you may need to remember it.

The good news is your leadership can pay dividends. Bad times and rough transitions usually do not last forever! This is a good time to review the work you have done in Part I and II, where you will find what it is that sparked you as a couple and you will find your family constitution and mission statements. Whatever collaboration, kindness, and expressions of love you can muster become important during these times. Often when progress appears, it comes slowly at first.

Marriage is about doing what is needed for yourself and your family. There are examples of marriages all around you that have gone through struggles and have made it. The couples are happy. They have figured out how to work together. Each person has had to change somehow. Often changing one's mind and saying "I'm wrong" or "I'm sorry" or forgiving has been the key. Another thing you might say is, "Let's try a different approach."

If you come to a place where there are no resolutions, it is probably time to go to therapy. It is much better to go to therapy early than late. What couples often find is that the slightest changes can be enough to keep a marriage workable for the moment and can begin the dialogue necessary for healing.

Sometimes doing the smallest things can keep love alive. A one or two percent change in intention, attitude or behavior is enough to make a dramatic, positive change in the whole marriage. The only problem is that most couples cannot see it or access it by themselves. Most marriage problems reside with both partners rather than just one. There are times when one person can participate in therapy and find the strength to accept what is a given and to create other positive changes.

Learning About The Way Marriage Is

Marriage is better than a fairy tale story. What you need to know is that, in spite of the ups and downs normal to marriage, both the tedious working through of differences and the enchanting, magical moments of your collaborations, your marriage is much better than any fairy tale could be. To be happy you will need to remember that marriage is not just a destination but also a journey. It is often too easy to blame your partner for something that is plain hard. Not everything that happens is your partner's fault. What I mean is marriage is rewarding and fulfilling and yet also a challenge. Do not blame your partner for this. It is the way life is. You are both learning. Try not to be too hard on each other.

There is a fooler aspect of marriage that you may have already discovered. You may have found that you care so much that you are sometimes lured into maddening, word-hurling battles. You may have said to yourself, "I've chosen the right guy (or I've chosen the right gal), so what's the problem?" If you didn't care, you would not argue. The question is, how do you fight in such a way that each of you still wind up being friends and lovers?

Even in common quarrels there is a temptation to run and tell on your spouse to someone who might be willing to listen to you. Don't do it if you can at all help yourself. And remember you are in a relationship. In most cases getting your way is not as important as finding common ground. Usually winning an argument is not as important as finding a way to work together.

If you come from a family where roles were distinctly drawn and each parent had their own way in their "arena of work," you may find that working things out with your partner seems strange. Learning to collaborate certainly takes time. Making an agreement that you may first disagree about without ending up enemies is important. Taking a time out from the arguing can be helpful. You may have heard the saying, "Never go to bed mad." Here is a word of wisdom. I assure you there will be a time of anger when either your best choice or your only choice will be to sleep on it. It is not an appealing solution. There are times when you may be so tired that things may not make sense. But carrying arguments forward without resolving them as quickly as you can is usually the best choice.

There are ways of working things out. If you are not in continuous conflict and you have a working relationship, then talking things over helps. You find that to any one action you or your partner may have more doubts, more "nos" than the other. There is a time when one partner needs to bow to the no of the other. There may be times when on a scale of one to twenty, each partner can rate how much doing something is important or not important. The partner who rates something higher may then get his or her way.

With time you learn how to work things out. With wisdom or perhaps through grace, you may come to realize that you do not truly change anybody. You have some power to change yourself. You will notice that your partner is changing as you are but not necessarily to your specifications. This is the critical part of the journey. The best scenario is to realize both of you can change, both of you can decide it is a good thing, and both of you can adjust to make your marriage work.

There comes a time in your changing that you will be forced to deal with your own insecurities and shortcomings. It will seem that your partner highlights these blemishes in you. Of course, the person you marry will inevitably bring your attention to the personal interior work you need to do. There is no escaping this. It happens in every marriage that your partner can help bring you to a point of frustration. It is not necessarily done in meanness. It is always almost inevitable in every marriage.

No one seems very happy at first to do interior work to somehow to deal with shortcomings, baggage, and so on. Your own work, regardless of how much interior baggage you are carrying, is not your problem. If you have a problem, it is the relationship (attitude or frame of mind) you choose to the work you have to do. Your situation shows up just as it is. Your relationship to it is the challenge you have. Believe it or not, it is very helpful knowing that you can change your relationship to a problem. Doing so can be helpful and emotionally healthy. Then you may find that the problem you think you have can sometimes change or resolve itself, and this experience is often very, very freeing.

About Therapy

There are two very good reasons to participate in therapy. One is you or your marriage has adverse problems that negatively affect you and your family's functioning. The other is that you believe with professional help you can develop ideas, approaches, or models that will accelerate your own growth or your family's growth. Change is usually a central topic in therapy.

Perhaps the toughest realization is neither person can successfully prescribe change in the other. Change cannot be dictated. However, even as people do change, the changes one might hope for are not guaranteed. Often the therapist can find a path to a positive change that may have been previously overlooked and underrated.

The topics facilitated by the therapist include how to communicate better and how to re-romanticize your marriage. Sometimes therapy and a marriage are energized by admitting mistakes, making an apology, and speaking one's own truth. Often this is easier to do with a therapist's help. It is surprising to some that a positive change formulated while in therapy in one contentious area can lead to positive changes in another.

What you individually or as a couple need to realize is there are problems even friends or relatives are not capable of handling. Sometimes the training and the insight of a professional therapist is the only alternative that can bridge gaps in understanding and help find solutions that can begin to change the direction of your family.

In therapy, rather than taking sides, the therapist focuses on healing the relationship. What is required from you as an individual or a couple is to take this situation as seriously as the therapist does. You will be asked to work on your problems. If you find yourself spending less time and expressing less interest in your situation than the therapist, it becomes obvious your intent for healing your relationship is substantially missing.

Often you as a couple are given homework assignments. You may be asked to play roles, keep a journal, and take on individual and mutual assignments. You may be asked to meet the therapist as a couple and then meet the therapist individually. The purpose of individual meetings is to clarify your personal issues that may be complicating your relationship.

Even the marriages with the most problems have a chance to be saved. There are some remaining good elements that make it possible for the couple to envision a future together. They often, though sometimes grudgingly, can admit that the other has some good qualities. It can be a starting place.

In marriages in which couples have had hugely bad experiences with one another, rebuilding the marriage, as if from scratch, is often necessary. The therapist will ask couples to do personal work that was not done either while they were dating or during the marriage.

The results are often very good. It is better to come to a therapist while both of you still think you want the marriage. Lives can be healed, marriages can be saved, and children can be protected.

However, often nothing happens when couples work on seemingly intractable problems without help. Sometimes lives are eventually healed and restored only after years of work. Sometimes a divorce is the only option. A time when divorce may be a good thing is when the marriage relationship has dissolved into "mutual warfare." Divorce is often not a good idea if there are other options available. However, if there is violence-in the rare cases of the woman beating up the man, or more often, when a man is beating a woman-that marriage is actually over.

Intoxication, while often adding to violence, is never an excuse for violence. Hanging on in this kind of crisis is living an illusion. Get out! If a woman and/or children are at risk from violence, the best approach is to get out now. FAST! If it is a man that is being abused, there is added shame because of false understanding of masculinity. The advice is the same. Get out! Find help, call a hotline, see a social worker, get out of the location, and go to relatives home or to a shelter. Don't wait.

Chapter 17

A Vision of Hope

 I am creating my marriage
with creativity, persistence and endurance
always finding the possibility of joy.

Chapter 17

*M*arriage can offer nurturing love and sustaining purpose. The adventure of marriage can be a wonderful and joyful experience. The good news is that marriage still works. There is possibility and hope for all marriages. When couples talk, think, and make decisions together, their marriages can prosper. Couples are often unprepared for marriage and have no way to deal with the issues with which they are confronted. This premise of this book is that inviting and challenging couples to give time and effort to the work of their marriage is the key to making it successful. If you hit snags, find yourself in a fight, and cannot figure out what the next step is, the worst thing to do, from my point of view, is to throw yourself into the arms of another. Usually being disloyal to your principles, to your understanding of marriage, and to your loved one will only complicate problems.

The amazing experience, the good results, the good feelings of working with your partner, your lover, are too often minimized. What you will surely discover is there is nothing like the experience and the bonding of trust, even in the doing of simple tasks when they are based on your mutual agreement, and when they work in same direction for the same goal. The power of being a couple, an item, a partnership, a powerful unit with purpose is powerful.

About Questions and Commitment

Your partner is the one who most likely knows your inner secrets and life struggles and yet loves you anyway and communicates with you with love and purpose every day. Do you get that? This is a trust relationship acted out in the nitty-gritty of everyday. This kind of understanding leads to a mutual, powerful intimacy for both of you.

Your partner can cause or precipitate a deep struggle in your own personal life and at same time help reveal a true awe that only committed lovers can know. It is at these points, when you feel as if you are in struggle or ecstasy, that you find out how profound of an effect your partner has on you. In moments of appreciation you have the pleasure of a deep breath and you can say, "I truly have found my soul mate."

In the midst of hope for the success of marriages, many young people have raised some staggering questions. I want to touch on these briefly because they are so important.

The first question many pose to their parents and to many of the older generation is about the viability of marriage. They have witnessed and often personally experienced the reality of divorce and they are unsure about marriage.

Many of you have told me that as you examined your parents' relationships, you have no hope or possibility of learning from them as positive role models for marriage. You have had to look at many more people to find the stories of successful marriage. Others have told me that you are in relationships, living together, but are afraid to commit to marriage because you are unsure that it will work for you. Others of you have said that you committed to marriage only after deciding to have children. Many of you who are living together report that although it may seem like a trial marriage, you and your partner generally are not in it to stay.

For those of you who have carefully read this book and participated in the full experience of this journey, you have become aware of how different the thinking about this adventure of marriage has become. Even today many people do not have the critical insight, or what we might call the profound knowledge, that is so critical to marriage success.

Let me say something here about struggles and failures of marriage. The so-called baby boom generation and the following generation have had a very high divorce rate. This needs to be talked about here because so many of you have long-abiding questions about your own relationship to marriage.

Divorce is not easy. Some of us honestly and forthrightly have taken personal responsibility for our own failures and finally for the divorce that ended our marriages. For many of us, it was not easy admitting that our great hope and passion would never ever work. Many of us have had those painful personal conversations with our children about how and why our marriages were ending.

Some of us have apologized to our children for the added burdens that divorce may have caused. Some of us experienced the great shame of not being able to keep our marriages together long enough to see our children into adulthood. For most of us, it was one of the most painful times of our lives.

However, what we also need to say to young people is that we as a generation, those of us who were a part of the fifty percent divorce rate, most often no longer understood the foundations that could make a marriage successful. As most of you who have read this book understand, there have been great shifts that took place in America and therefore inevitably marriage relationships also dramatically changed. It frankly caught most of us by surprise. We, as married couples, have been so focused on the problems that each of us caused in our own marriages that we did not understand the great shifts in America that blindsided our relationships.

More than the advent of more women working jobs, more than the advances of birth control, more than the real revolution that was created by the automatic washer and dryer, something else rocked marriages. It was the reconstitution of our communities, after World War II; it was a time in which we became strangers to one another as we moved into our new homes and in our new neighborhoods. In this new construction of American life, when so many people moved every five to seven years, usually there were no grandparents, aunts, and uncles close by to support our marriages and help raise our kids. In other words, marriages changed when people moved from their rural communities to a place where no one knew you, and very few in the community at large cared whether our individual marriages succeeded.

So to you who are approaching marriage and realize that it is a new reality, you are smarter and wiser about relationships. You may realize that all of your friends may not have grounded, real wisdom about marriage themselves. For those of you who have accepted advice about relationships from friends about how your marriage is doing, it is worth taking pause and embracing a healthy skepticism.

Many of your friends will never be invested in the journey of your happiness and intimacy. If you are fortunate, some will. Frankly most people in the towns and neighborhoods before World War II did not necessarily understand how important they were to marriage. They simply lived the way they lived and did what they did.

Unlike the communities of yesteryear that were a part of country life, small towns and close-knit neighborhoods that included family and lifelong friends. Many people who may be your friends today know you in a much different way. You may refer to them for wisdom about your personal life, and they may not in the long run be invested in your success.

So, what you know and how you speak and act has taken on a new importance in marriage. It is a shift from a strong, socially supportive framework of life to one in which the knowledge you have, the psychology of marriage, so to speak, becomes hugely important.

Because the knowledge factor in marriage is so important, I encourage you to revisit some major themes from the book to help you gain insight into what makes a successful relationship:

- Engagement is not merely a time to plan the wedding. It is the time to look ahead and to plan your marriage.

- Creating trust is a major factor in building a successful relationship and an all-important foundation in marriage.

- Your marriage partnership becomes strong when you embrace communication and make communication safe between you.

- The sociological supports for marriage, once taken for granted, are usually not available to couples. Today marriage is more about psychology and less about social support. Therefore, what you know, how you think, and how you communicate have become very important.

- Marriage inevitably is not only about creating your family but also about creating and participating in community.

- Speaking your truth to one another is a powerful and much better approach than putting on an act for each other or somehow trying to protect each other from truth.

- Being involved and making decisions together rather than simply always taking someone else's advice are keystones to building a powerful relationship.

- Learning to suspend judgment and to avoid trampling on each other's vulnerabilities helps create a solid and trusting foundation for your marriage.

- It is important to anticipate the ending of your first phase of romantic feelings after about the second year of your relationship and to look forward to learning and expressing a deeper more committed sense of love.

- You will feel frustrated in your marriage. Know that your partner will help create a situation in which you will be forced to do your own interior, personal work. This situation is a part of love. You may think, "How dare the one I love highlight the baggage I'm carrying." This can be a time of crisis if you choose to make it a crisis.

- However, the events leading to your facing your own internal baggage are usually inadvertent. In other words, this is something that happens in all marriages. Usually this occasion of frustrations is not a plot created by your partner.

- Marriage is not a competitive sport. It is, instead, the arena of cooperation and creativity. It is about a win-win outcome. This concept, win-win, is not well recognized in our society. Marriage is not about one partner winning and the other losing.

- A major goal of every marriage is to learn to get past the competitive conflict stage and move your relationship into the arena of mutual understanding, cooperation, collaboration, and teamwork.

- Every couple faces the inescapable work of finding community and/or creating community. This is not an idea supported by the "common sense" of society. That is, most people do not talk about building community when they talk about marriage. Helping to build community will nevertheless require some of your time and energy.

- We know that goals and mission are much more than religious or military concepts. How you are focused and how you are human matters. So here is a concept to try out in your life: Every person and every couple needs someone to love (at minimum each other, of course), work to do, and a great noble cause bigger than themselves to believe in-a cause that is larger than any one person could ever accomplish.

- Forgiveness is always a necessity in marriage.

- Communication that expresses love and gratitude can take place in many forms. Sex is important and talking about it is very important. And it is always helpful to say an authentic thank you every day.

- If you have children, do not give up your adult or parental responsibilities to your children individually or in a family meeting. Be careful not to let children make the adult decisions that belong to you. You are the parents, the adults. Adult discussion about adult issues needs to take place in private-usually away from the kids and, say, in your partners' meeting-wherever you decide that is.

○ There will be a time in every marriage where leadership and persistence in resolving problems will matter.

○ The act of cheating on your spouse also involves cheating on yourself.

○ The number one reason for divorce is that you, one or both partners, are more interested in winning and being right than you are in building a mutual marriage relationship.

○ Cooperation, not competition, is the dominant style that makes marriage work.

○ If your marriage is rocked by discord, it is much better to get therapy or counseling help early than to wait it out to the bitter end and then pray that a professional will save your marriage. Marriage counseling often fails when couples are too hard-headed to get timely help.

○ The point of mutuality, cooperation, and collaboration is to build the basis for intimacy. It is also to recognize that the two of you are unique and therefore need to build your own relationship, rather than relying on outside sources to tell you what your relationship needs to be.

○ Learning to be on the same financial page, knowing one another's values, and making mutual goals and spending targets is an unbelievably powerful way to give marriage a strong foundation.

○ It is good to reflect on stereotypes and old marriage roles to have a better understanding of what might not work. One approach-one idea-that generally does not work is in objectifying your partner. For example, women, including your wife, are not actually sex objects and are not perpetual fantasy playmates. Men, including your husband, are not "money objects" and are not perpetual ATM machines there for your personal use.

○ For those partners who have a mental incapacity, and there are more than we recognize, getting help from a professional is a necessary action to help make your marriage work.

○ To those of you, especially young adults, who seek the perfect partner and look for assurance from a Mr. or Ms. Right, hoping to find unconditional love from that person, I want to encourage you to realize that both happiness and love are daily decisions. This kind of thing-that is, to be in love and happy-depends more on what you individually decide than does strictly depending on your spouse to bring you love and happiness. Each of you has this responsibility. Usually the understanding, kindness, and daily decision to love is what is associated with the words unconditional love. It is about loyalty and continuing kindness. However, again, these depend on your daily decisions. It is good advice to fall in love with your partner every day.

To learn to stop, to take a breath is important. Rushing into arguments is usually not the best approach. Inevitably one or both of you will say something that is offensive. Think about it. Is this other person not your lover, your best friend, the one with whom you have shared your secrets and the one whose character you have admired in the past? There are usually two ways to take on offensive words. One is to interpret them as being negative and the other is to find the best meaning. I encourage you to find the best meaning. There will be time to deal with this issue if you turn out to be wrong.

With all of the books, workshops, and discussions about the divorce rate of the last half-century, there has been critical help for individuals. However, not one of these efforts has had the effect of stemming the divorce rate. Many things are found to be helpful-marrying later in life, having a steady job when marrying, having more years of education rather than less. All of these can but are not guaranteed to make a difference.

It appears that marriages must be made to work one marriage at a time and the couple's own knowledge or psychology is the biggest factor in marriage success. You, the two of you, working together are the key to happiness and marital success. The great thing about marriage is you may experience more happiness, better health, better sex, the possibility and joy of having children, legal recognition as a couple, overall physical and psychological intimacy, and the power of personal partnership.

My wish for you is that you may find joy, collaboration, thrill, and success in your relationship and your marriage. Not only is your happiness involved but so is the well-being of your community. Finally, if you become parents, the happiness of your children depends on your well-being as a couple.

Couple's Pose

Couples sitting in this position experience safety in communication. In this intimate connection it is helpful to first tell your lover how much you appreciate the gifts your partner brings into your life. It is a perfect time to say the genuine compliments and small thank yous for support given that day.

These actions then are a platform in which "I-statements" may be said. It is a place meant to express support, request help, and create intimate win-win outcomes. When done well this is a great foundation for even more physical intimacy.

Starter Question Index

Acknowledgements

This book was partly inspired by the work of the Ecumenical Institute and its course, Cultural Studies (CS) III-A, Family and the Individual. This innovative course was developed in the 1960s to fill a large gap that existed at that time, especially with the understanding that churches had about marriage, in furthering the understanding of how a marriage is enlivened by spirit and mission.

The participants were asked to do both in classwork and homework, and to record that work in a family album that reflected the couples' important values and insights. This course reflected the innovative genius of the Institute's Dean, Joseph Matthews, and the talented people that surrounded him. In publishing material, without any copyright, The Institute hoped to benefit individuals and the church at large and anyone else who might be able to use its material.

Consequently, the approaches, methods, and materials developed by the Institute are now used all over the world in businesses, schools, governments, and religious organizations, and of course some families. The idea of the family album originated long before there was a CS-IIIA course. Not only is the album a natural vehicle to record significant past events, it also can be a place to capture and keep safe a couple's visionary future dreams.

This book introduces workbook questions which, when answered, will allow you as a couple to create your own couple's book or album. This may also be done electronically. While utilizing the album concept, *After the Wedding Cake* moves substantially beyond the album's original context to offer help in vital marriage arenas such as communication, relations with in-laws, family money issues, and sex.

I am grateful to psychiatrist Dr. Domeena Renshaw, whose work in couples' therapy eventually led to the establishment of a clinic for couples with sexual dysfunction at Chicago's Loyola Hospital, located in Maywood, Illinois. Her work influenced the development of this book's chapter on sexuality. One of Dr. Renshaw's great insights was that couples who can deal successfully with sexual problems also can find it much easier to resolve all the other relationship issues.

ACKNOWLEDGEMENTS

David Dunn, a special friend, and a wonderful author/poet, encouraged and coached me. With his insistence I removed much of the "therapist's passive voice" from this text. Marge Philbrook, personal friend and Institute of Cultural Affairs legend, not only contributed insights and editing talent to this book, she has lived in and modeled the spiritual love that is also reflected in this book. Another neighbor. Maeve Lawler, now deceased, engaged me in a challenging bantering style conversation through which the title of this book emerged. Author Susan Barry, a North Carolina poet, and playwright generously gave both enthusiastic support and precious time to nudge my writing toward greater clarity. I owe a special thanks to my general editor Melanie Eckner, my designer Mickey Mankus, and illustrator Michael Coon, all of whom gave special effort and insight to this book.

Friends and neighbors have read drafts of this work and enthusiastically commented on its ideas. I am deeply grateful for those who have read and encouraged this work including, George Packard, Dick West, Kari Aosoved, the Rev. Jean Darling. I appreciate Dennis King's catching enthusiasm and vision that this book fulfills a need not yet met, even with all of the existing advice books on marriage.

I am also indebted to communities of people who have lent insight, especially the faculty at Loyola University Chicago Graduate School of Social Work, and support and encouragement, including clients, therapists, and social workers, friends, the Warriors of the Men's Movement, including Jack Chapman, Dennis King, and David Lindgren, and the larger learning community associated with the Ecumenical Institute. All of these people have cast themselves into the dynamic of the human servant force, have led by example, and pioneered healing initiatives for their communities, their families, and their own lives.

One of the big ideas in this book is that couples create their own couple's book. This idea is not new but the energized version of this idea from the Ecumenical Institute inspired much of my approach. Not only is the book or album, as it were, a natural vehicle to record significant past events, it also can be a place to capture and keep safe a couple's visionary future dreams.

I greatly appreciate my friend and colleague, theologian John Cock, author of *Jesus Christ for the 21st Century*, who shared the idea of self-starter question format with me.

Afterword

This is not an academic book. Instead it is a book that invites you the reader to participate in relationship-building thoughts and exercises. The book's premise is that the secret to strong marriage is an empowered couple who engage in full communication and make informed, mutual decisions. It is my intention to help thousands of people and bring a sense of stability and security.

No one else could have written this book. This book brings together many streams of thought, some of which comes from my own lived experience. Much of the information comes from what any therapist can learn and experience. I owe much to friends, experts, and practitioners in the work of therapy and couples work.

Many streams of thought that have influenced this book including those that come from my decade in a family religious order, the Order: Ecumenical. Here I learned about compassion, gratitude, covenantal living as well as service to others. There are also streams of thought that come from the Institute of Cultural Affairs, which taught me facilitation methods and enabled me to grow into a strong sense of community advocacy and community organization.

Another stream of thinking comes from my involvement in the last thirteen years in men's work with the Mankind Project and Path to Spirit Warrior, both of which insist on strong service to community and ethical living. I have been a member of a men's group for more than a decade and a facilitator in the PTSW training weekends. It is in this work that the tenets of truth-telling, integrity, responsibility, and accountability have emerged for me as powerful guides to whole-hearted living and have helped inform my understanding of personal and family life. I strive to emulate those ideals.

When I started working in human services, it was my goal to help many hundreds of people. When I worked, under a special grant, for the Community Counseling Centers of Chicago, I was given the assignment to work in an Uptown, Chicago circuit in which I would do assessments, on the spot counseling, make referrals for professional help, and on occasion hospitalize those who had become too sick to cope. It was during these rounds of thirteen weekly Uptown destinations that included a health clinic, four different homeless drop-in shelters, four homeless overnight shelters, and four Single Resident Occupancy buildings, that ideas for this book started to emerge. In a month's time I would interview anywhere from 80 to 120 people. There was always a great satisfaction of making a positive difference in peoples' lives.

It was on these rounds, as I worked in the Salvation Army Family Shelter and the Cornerstone Shelter, that I met couples and their children who had lost their jobs, their homes, and their hopes, and sometimes their health. Before coming to the shelter, many had tried to survive any way they could, even by living in their cars or camping in a park. The couples were desperate to know that their children would be okay and, even in the shock of having lost everything, they wanted to know if they would come out of this tragedy and be okay as couples. As I talked with many of them, I came to realize that there was much about life pertaining to marriage that they did not know. Many had a weak grounding in understanding their relationships. I do not say that if they had been better prepared for marriage, the unemployment disaster that overtook this country could have been avoided. What occurred to me was that, when crisis hit, these couples knew so little about themselves and their marriages. This consciousness was the turning point and the inspiration for this book.

Another stream of thought comes from my lived experience as I struggled to keep two marriages together, one of 23 years and one of 7; I finally came to the nearly untenable realization that I had failed. I have spent many hours working through the successes and great wonderful times in these marriages and looking for and examining the factors that were destructive to them. Here I have seen my own shortcomings and taken stock of my part in these. I have looked for answers and worked through the lessons that these reflections have taught me. This also included examining issues of illness that befell my relationships. It is a painful reality to share these truths with you, the reader, but it is out of this experience, and not just clinical social work, that a lot of insight has come for this book.

My children, three daughters, remain the most precious gift I have been given. I have five grandchildren I adore immensely and to whom this book is dedicated. I live in Chicago and although I am semi-retired, I continue on in men's work and couples therapy. I hope this book makes a huge difference in the life of anyone who undertakes the path laid out in it.

May you experience continued love and intimacy in your relationship.

Ed Feldmanis

Annotated Bibliography

Bourne, Edmund J. (2005). *The anxiety & phobia workbook*. Oakland, CA: New Harbinger Publications.This is one of many accessible books helping people work through mental challenges. The idea here is that responsibility starts with the individual but is also a challenge for which there is professional help.

Brown, Brené. (2013, September 21). *Brené Brown: Listening to shame*. [Video file] Retrieved from http://www.ted.com/talks/brene_brown_listening_to_shame.html This great TED Talk by Brené Brown is very accessible. Once people catch on to her ideas, communication can become much easier. She helps people understand how to be safe and yet vulnerable.

Brown, Brené. (2012). *Daring greatly: how the courage to be vulnerable transforms the way we live, love, parent, and lead.* New York, NY: Gotham. Many people raise the question of what is meant by "doing your own personal work." Dr. Brown answers this question with beautiful and simple explanations. She is courageous in sharing her own life experiences. After encountering Dr. Brown's works, the reader can comprehend what is meant by not depending on your "act" but instead being the real you.

Chapman, Gary D. (2009). *The five love languages*. Chicago, IL: Northfield Pub. This book opens the wider definition of communication to include loving behaviors.

Comfort, Alex. (2009). *The joy of sex* (Rev. ed.). New York: Crown. This is an updated version of an earlier book that created raves of acclamation across the country. It is one of the first couples books to explore many facets of how to be sexy. In a time when most couples had limited access to information, Alex Comfort illustrated the fun of sex.

Corn, Laura. (2005). *101 nights of grrreat romance: secret sealed seductions for fun-loving couples.* Santa Monica, CA: Park Avenue Publishers, Inc. This author also created the Great American Sex Diet. In her books she includes spicy couples' to dos, adventures, dares, and romantic encounters. Her works are well worth reading and most of her prescriptions are enjoyable and doable. 101 Nights of Grrreat Romance pushes an edgier sexy spirit, which is somewhat daring. Her works are very couple-friendly.

Corn, Laura. (2008). *101 sexy dares.* New York: Simon Spotlight Entertainment.

Corn, Laura. (2016). *Seductions and 101 Nights.* (downloadable app) Retrieved from: http://101nights.com. This is the best-selling author's digital launch to satisfy fans having special occasions and nneding ideas right away.

Covey, Stephen R. (2005). *The 8th habit: from effectiveness to greatness.* New York: Free Press. This book explains how to develop a creative, authentic voice in challenging situations. Stephen Covey promotes fair dealing and character in business and personal life. He popularized and added insight to the ideas of personal and family mission as well as effectively described the new win-win mindset not understood by many, helping people understand true collaboration and teamwork. This book is updated from the previous *Seven Habits of Highly Effective People.* Covey's genius has at times been positively compared to that of the great W. Edwards Deming.

Covey, Stephen R. (1990). *The seven habits of highly effective people: powerful lessons in personal change.* New York: Simon and Schuster. Dr. Covey, who wrote for families and for business, popularized ideas of mission and a new style of listening in his works. His time management and planning tools for individuals are also highly popular.

Douglass, Marcia, & Douglass, Lisa. (1996). *Are we having fun yet?: The intelligent woman's guide to sex.* New York: Hyperion. This is a couple-friendly book. The title is somewhat misleading but the authors are brilliant. This is a serious book for both men and women. These two professional women, also sisters, clarify sexual issues for women while at the same time lovingly honor men and witness to the possibilities of intimacy. They tackle harmful and misleading sex myths in this work.

  After the Wedding Cake

Fanning, Patrick, & O'Neill, John T. (1996). *The addiction workbook.* Oakland, CA: New Harbinger Publications.
An important and accessible work to help dismantle hard addictions, which is very necessary work for many in order to save relationships. Often people who find this book helpful would find a talk therapist helpful as well.

Fritz, Sandra (with Mosby Editorial Board). (1996). *Mosby's visual guide to massage essentials.* St. Louis: Mosby.
One of the important and necessary elements in a successful marriage is to take an active interest in health and to create family modalities of health. Massage is a health practice that can also be available to families.

Hallowell, Edward M., & Ratey, John J. (2005). *Delivered from distraction: getting the most out of life with attention deficit disorder.* New York: Ballantine.
Great for families who have a person with Attention Deficit Disorder. This is a ground-breaking work by two Harvard psychiatrists, both of whom have ADD or, as otherwise known, ADHD. Their work changed medicine, and therapy for, as well as the self-understanding of, this mental challenge.

Hendrix, Harville. (2008). *Getting the love you want: a guide for couples* (Rev. ed.). New York: Harper Perennial.
Dr. Hendrix moves readers from a self-centered idea of relationship to one of sharing responsibility and sharing communication.

Hendrix, Harville. (1992). *Keeping the love you find: a guide for singles.* New York: Pocket Books.
Dr. Hendrix has influenced therapy and many allied or associated professionals working with couples. His insights are used by numerous therapists.

Hooper, Anne. (2009). *Anne Hooper's ultimate sex positions: over 100 positions for maximum erotic pleasure* (Rev. ed.). New York: DK Publishing.
This book is for those hot moments when you just can't get enough of each other as a couple. Originally released in 1992, this book brought Ms. Hooper, well-respected sex therapist, to the public's attention.

Hyman, Bruce M., & Pedrick, Cherry. (2005). *The OCD workbook: breaking free from obsessive compulsive disorder.* Oakland, CA: New Harbinger Publications.
One of many workbooks available to deal with mental challenges. For some, not getting help and not doing personal work can mean the end to marriage.

After the Wedding Cake 211

McDonald, Kathleen. (2005). *How to meditate.* Boston: Wisdom Publications. A representative book of an explosive arena of literature, this book introduced a family health modality that any family can use to bring stability to their lives. Meditation can be an effective family health modality and is useful in doing what I refer to in this book as interior work.

Nichols, Michael P. (2013). *Family therapy: concepts and methods* (10th ed.). Boston, MA: Pearson.
This book highlights how therapy can help if couples have the courage to engage in it earlier rather than later.

Orman, Suze. (2011). *The money class: learn to create your new American dream.* New York: Spiegel & Grau.
Suze Orman is probably one of the best-known financial advisors. She has solid knowledge and provides good money advice. All of her books are well worth the time and effort.

Ramsey, Dave. (1998). *The financial peace planner.* New York: Penguin Books.
This author is particularly helpful, unlike some who do not understand the time value of money. He is included here solely because he is a pioneer in speaking to people who are not rich: the so-called average man and woman. Mr. Ramsey is personally capable of figuring out the six factors of 1 and explaining very well these time-money concepts.

Ramsey, Dave. (2003). *The total money makeover.* Nashville: Thomas Nelson Publishers.
This Nashville-based, populistic financial guru insists on attacking debt and creating potent savings programs.

Ruiz, Miguel, & Mills, Janet. (2008). *The four agreements.* San Rafael, CA: Amber-Allen Publishing.
This is not a marriage manual but the basic wisdom in this book can successfully guide individuals and couples past marriage-wrecking disagreements.

Ruiz, Miguel, Ruiz, Jose Luis, with Mills, Janet. (2010). *The fifth agreement: a practical guide to self-mastery.* San Rafael, CA: Amber-Allen Pub.
This book essentially discusses all five agreements including those of the earlier book: keep your word and use it to build up relationships, don't take it personally, don't assume, do your best, be skeptical-listen deeply to learn.

Renshaw, Domeena. (1995). *Seven weeks to better sex* (2nd ed.). New York: Random House & American Medical Association.
The author is based in the Chicago area and is an early pioneer in sex education and therapy. She is beloved by many who attribute the saving of their marriages to her efforts. She is someone this author has known personally. Her sexual dysfunctions clinic always had a year's backlog on the waiting list.

Rubin, Theodore I. (1998). *The angry book.* New York: Simon and Schuster.
The author, a psychiatrist, created a groundbreaking understanding of how to make anger a friend rather than an enemy. He was one of the few who early distinguished anger from rage and taught people how to handle and live with one and eliminate the other.

Stanfield, Bryan R. (Ed.) (2006). *The art of focused conversation: 100 ways to access group wisdom in the workplace.* Gabriola Island, B.C.: New Society Publishers.
Although this book is written for businesses and organizations, it is an easy way to learn an advanced communication skills. This work complements my appendix section on advanced communication for couples.

Vanzant, Iyanla. (2013). *Forgiveness: 21 days to forgive everyone for everything.* Carlsbad, CA: Smiley Books / Hay House.
Author captures the sense of why forgiveness is necessary and why it is important. In the final analysis this can be the key to making marriage work.

Winfrey, Oprah, & Robertson, Terri L. (Ed.). (2008). *O's big book of happiness: the best of O, the Oprah Magazine: wisdom, wit, advice, interviews, and inspiration.* Birmingham, Ala.: Oxmoor House.
Oprah offers stories and ideas that are about authentic living. Truth Telling. These stories are heart-warming and necessary lessons about being the real you. It is the real you that needs to show up in marriage.

Wynn, Claire. (2006). *Simply reflexology: reduce stress, increase energy and improve your overall wellbeing.* Heatherton, Australia: Hinkler Books Pty Ltd.
This amazing book teaches another arena of family health modalities.

 The Sign of Jumis
This sign represents the wheat stalk,
a symbol of abundance and growth.
It is the outcome, the very fruit of planting,
nurturing and weeding.

As you embark on expanding your own skills,
adopting tools that build good relationships,
may you enjoy the good outcomes
that come from mindful work.

Appendix

Appendix I

The Study Guide:
Twelve Weeks to Planning Your Successful Marriage

WEEK I:
PREPARATION

Focus Question: What preparation do we need (do I need) to begin our work?

Tools: An album, memory book, scrapbook, or its electronic equivalent is needed to help with thinking and reflection.

Discussion: If you follow these suggestions, you will have a history of your romantic experience. This is what you will go back to, you will refer to, to remember what you said and who you are. You may not know it now, but this can and likely will become an important tool in your marriage.

Assignment: This is an adventure with a little bit of work. It is about creating the story about you-you personally and you as a couple. Talk about how to do this journey-thinking with your partner. Make a commitment: Decide you will not just have an ordinary marriage, but that you will take the leap to go for excellence. You will undertake making the decisions that will help ensure your love. Decide to jump in and go for love and intimacy and learn to keep the love and intimacy that belongs to you.

So ... create your couple's book with your partner. I encourage you to write down what you discuss in these twelve weeks and make them a part of your physical or electronic album. Make a general plan of how the two of you might spend time together creating your book. Special note: It is okay for one of you to be more in charge of guiding this process. It is not okay to have one of you drop out of decision making. You are a couple together and you, together, can and should make your own road map of marriage.

Begin gathering photographs and mementoes and other items that help tell your story; this will make starting your book easy. The first part is about you and about your love. Put these in place where you can find them. Find or buy a memory book, album, or scrapbook in which you can keep writings, photos, drawings, and other such items.

Not only can you relive some of the excitement of how you met and how you became a couple, you will have a reference to guide you. You will have them in your own couple's book.

WEEK II:
THE BEGINNING OF SHARING YOUR LOVE STORY

Focus Question: What are the events and experiences that have made us the couple, the unit, we are? (In other words, what are all the things that made me fall head over heels in love? What is it that makes us click as a couple?)

Discussion: This is the time you will read or review Part One, the first chapters of this book. Let this book be your guide in putting together your thoughts. You will have a chance to organize your memory items, like tickets from your great movie date, the picture from the party, or an item from where you first met. You can write a short description and add these things to your own book. Don't be totally surprised that you might find memories that are pretty hot. Also you may experience confidence both about doing this work and who you are as a couple.

Assignment: Read the first four chapters. Pull from the book all that seems applicable to you. Explain by writing short statements in your own words about how and why you are in love. Your participation with each other also helps your thinking. It helps in making decisions about your relationship and can be a critical factor to your being A GREAT COUPLE. Discuss with each other how you are compatible, how you fell in love, and what it is that makes you a couple. There a specific questions and to-dos in the book. Organize material you have and make sure important descriptions are written.

Keeping the ideas just discussed in mind, to follow up and help complete your work, use the Starter Questions in Chapter 4: Capturing and Sharing Your Special Moments.

Remember that the questions are there so that you cover all the important points. Not all questions need to be answered in order. Reflect on whether you have written down what's important to you. Anytime that you feel inspired to add a page or break up your text with an illustration like a photograph, feel free to do that. Remember to add a note or caption that explains the illustration.

WEEK III:
MARRIAGE ROLE MODELS

Focus Question: What are the gifts of knowledge and wisdom that friends and family offer about great marriages? Who are marriage role models?

Discussion: The last assignment was about how you got together and what that has meant to you. This assignment, still in Chapter Four, has Starter Questions about Accessing Wisdom of Friends and Family. You are encouraged to look at how friends, neighbors, and other family members conduct their relationship.

Assignment: Collect your thoughts. See if you have three families that could be role models for you. Write about them and then say what you learned from their relationship. Here are a some pointers: Are there moments when friends and family did particularly loving things? Were there times when you admired their courage? Find out what you can learn from them and each other. Please read these Starter Questions to see what they might inspire for you.

WEEK IV:
FAMILY, HISTORY, TRADITIONS

Focus Question: Who are the immediate families in our lives? What are their backgrounds, traditions, and important life events? What can you learn as a couple from each of your family histories?

Discussion: This is similar to the last assignment, but this one is about focusing on specific history, traditions, and important stories. In many ways you are the family you come from. Take to heart the best of this history.

Assignment: The Starter Questions here are about Your Family, Relatives, and Background. Check out the questions. Capture ideas about how holidays are celebrated, what traditions, if any, guide your families. Look for things that have happened or your families have done for which they express pride. This would be a good time to fill in any knowledge gaps about your family history and how you relate to your family. Please read the Starter Questions. Please include a narrative of the best you have learned from your families and how you see yourselves differently.

WEEK V:
YOUR FAMILY SYMBOL

Focus Question: Who are you? How do you say who you are with an image, as a piece of art, as a symbol?

Discussion: This assignment could not come first because it requires the kind of reflection that has taken place in the first four weeks. This is a creation piece that you make. It is your art. Will it be like a "family crest" or shield? Will it be a plaque on the door? Will it be in the form of a circle, square, rectangle? Is it something you can frame and hang up?

Sometimes people have taken something from their geography, the location where they live, and have said this particular part of their landscape reminds them how they are grounded and rooted as a family. Others have taken some other symbol, something familiar, and re-created it as their own.

This is a time to think about the conversations you have had; there have been many and they have been deep sharing. What did you learn about who you are as a couple? What from your experience, your dating, tells you who you are? Is there something in your common background or common spirituality that speaks to your identity? For instance, do you have sacred objects?

Assignment: Start where your imagination has already taken you. Do whatever you need to get your idea shaped up. Make a decision. Don't be afraid to make a mistake. Jump into this assignment. For those of you who might be more perfectionistic, well, I hope you are not screaming at this assignment. Nevertheless, here is what is asked of you. Whether you are completely sure or not about what creative thing or art represents and symbolizes you, don't worry. It is more important to do something, to make something. It is the start that teaches us and makes the difference.

Some of you may have the light bulb go off in your heads. You know what piece you need and what you will make.

For those just experimenting and making something for the first time: this is supposed to be at least a little bit challenging, and that's okay, so don't worry about that. Choose something important in your lives: A tree, for example, or some other meaningful thing, maybe something musical, or something spiritual. Use its picture. Try out putting your family name at the top of the picture: the Abenaa Family, the Smith Family, for example. Then at the sides or bottom, try putting guiding words that represent who you are; maybe words that are important to you. See if this idea works for you. This is a suggestion about how to experiment with this. By the way, you may or may not even need extra words in your symbol.

There are a lot of things that can go into a family symbol. It does not have to be complicated. But ... if you don't start and do this, you won't have one. Oh, someone might say, this is our family "brand." Well, maybe, but family symbols have been around a much longer time.

WEEK VI:
Promises: Public and Personal Covenants

Focus Question: What is it you promise each other in marriage?

Discussion: Your focus is now being shifted from all of the objective facts and foundational information about how you show up as a couple to point you into a new reflection about your relationship. The context of this assignment is that you will be thinking about the first two covenants of marriage. Those are the public vows and the private vows. One is formal. The other is shaped by you as lovers, and is about how you honor each other, and how you are intimate together. In this book we describe the four covenants of marriage. This week is about the first two covenants.

Assignment: Start by looking at the bigger picture. First, take the time to talk with each other about what marriage means to you. What is it about being married that is important? What is your image of living together and spending time together?

Now talk through why you love each other, why you cherish being together, what it is that is precious in your relationship. Then each of you write these down. This is a starting point of understanding your promises to keep.

Next take a look at the public covenant. If you are a member of a religious institution, the covenant of marriage is easy to find. It can often be found online or in your book of hymns and worship. Read this covenant together. Discuss what it means to you.

For most couples there is a degree of nervousness in being part of the whole marriage ceremony. And possibly, as is the case with many couples, the covenant recognized by your own faith may be just fine for you. Others, a few, write their own marriage vows, and some faiths allow this. For those of you who do not have an affiliation, there are marriage covenants, vows, on the internet. You can download one of these.

Read the covenant. Take this opportunity to highlight what you as a couple are committed to and grasp what vows of marriage are all about. You can ask questions and talk about what you want in your marriage. This is the time to compare your personal inspirations, those ideas about how you cherish each other, and discuss these comparing them to the public covenant. Make a copy of this covenant for your couple's book.

The second part: What is not in your covenant that you want and need to say? You may find that your sentiments and loving thoughts are only generally represented in the public covenant. Get clear on what is not said in the covenant. Those sentiments and wonderful sweet ideas can then be the foundation to shape your private covenant.

You have the public covenant. So now write out your personal covenant. It does not need to be long. Here are some ideas that may be included: How are you friends and what is it about your friendship that you want to continue to nurture during your marriage? What is your commitment to communicating with one another? What are your ideas about loyalty, faithfulness, and support you have in common? How do you see forgiveness playing a role?

You may also want to discuss even more personal things. This is your private covenant. What does intimacy mean to you? How do you plan to be sexual together? (Sex in this context can mean how you commit time and attention to one another; how you are open to communicating needs to each other; and how, when it is necessary, the two of you bring up and resolve questions about your sex practices.) Add whatever you write down to your couples book.

WEEK VII:
Your Family and Community

Focus Question: Why is it necessary to know yourself and understand your family in a relationship to community?

Discussion: Most weddings take place with a brief understanding of the public vows, sometimes introduced by a minister and practiced at a wedding rehearsal. Believe it or not, in a much simpler time in America, this was often enough. Times change and yet for many, not much more attention is given to vows. If in fact you completed the review of the public covenant and created a private one, you are a galaxy ahead in preparation for marriage.

What has also changed is the communities themselves. Most people live far away from other family and do not have many friends nearby with whom friendship has developed over a lifetime. There are very few people around you who are really invested in the success of your marriage. You are about to risk marriage, and you may be about having children. You certainly are conscious about how many marriages fail.

This situation has taken place, for example, because there have been major economic and sociological changes in this country. Without a tight network supporting marriage, many marriages have failed. In this context what you know and how you behave becomes more important. At the same time your family will need to make all kinds of connections and will likely need more than the resources that most communities can offer.

Since it is probably true that no one, especially since the end of World War in your city or neighborhood will help you define who you are and who y family is, it is work that you will need to do. You are now invited to creat personal mission statement. Who are you in relationship to your community? What do you do?

This covenant has two parts. The first is the creation of a personal mission statement for yourself. This statement is one you share with each other. So this is yet another invitation to risk something. One risk is that you write something that is wrong. Another is that you write something that later will embarrass you.

I have seen brave smart people wither at this simple job. There are many excuses like, "I feel as if I failed and I will have to write something wrong." Or "I really don't know myself and I am only now figuring it out. So I don't know what to say."

If you find this task frightening, I have to ask you, "Are you really in love? Are you ready for marriage knowing it is a risk?" Usually if you write something, it turns out surprisingly better then you thought it would. So write something out. Make a draft. Get a start.

Assignment: Whether you follow someone's formula or you figure out things differently does not matter. Suggestion: Imagine who you will be in five years. Name it. If that is fairly clear, then the next thing to do is to add action to it. You just may have created a great personal mission statement.

If you are stuck, go to the Internet and download mission statements. Then read these. Ask how these statements represent you. You will find many that do not connect to who you are. This begins to tell you what to write for yourself. If you are really desperate and do not know what to do, find one that is most likely close to who you are. See if you can live with it and what you can learn.

WEEK VIII:
THE FAMILY MISSION STATEMENT

Focus Question: What are our commitments as a couple, as a family to ourselves and community?

Discussion: The second part of this covenant is to create a family mission. Together with your individual mission statement, you will have a covenant as it relates to you as a couple and to the larger community. Say what you are about, how you are together, how you show up in community, and how you relate to and build community. Each family's statement will be different. The statement should contain aspects of you and community, some relationship as mission, as it is important to you.

Assignment: Here again write down your notions. Think about living in a place you want to be. What then does that community need from you? If you have children, what is it about community that is important to you?

Write something down now. This may take longer than the first statement. The difference is the first time you were writing your own statement in cooperation with each other. Now you are writing one statement together.

If you need help go to the Internet and download family mission statements. As before, compare and contrast these with your reality. You will find things to say that represent who you are.

WEEK IX:
THE FAMILY CONSTITUTION

Focus Question: How do you organize yourself, make decisions and operate as a family?

Discussion: Earlier there were exercises and specific questions about your observations of other couples and families. This is your opportunity to take your own understanding of how families work and combine the knowledge you gained from observing others. An outline of one family constitution is available to you as a guide. In the previous set of Starter Questions you were asked about your compatibility, ability to forgive, and how you intend to keep your romance alive. Let the answers to those questions guide you as well.

Assignment: Plunge in, decide what sections your constitution will have and write a paragraph for each section. If there are agreed ways you have decided to talk with one another (your couple's communication) or principles about how to organize your time, include them as well somewhere in your constitution. Use the sample outline to start your own thinking.

Here is a sample outline:

I. Preamble: Forming a Partnership in Love with Trust and Fidelity

II. Our Financial Guidelines: The Who, What, and Where of Making Our Money and Family Work; Financial Partners in Good Times and Bad

III. Our Family Decision Making, The Partner Meeting, The Family Meeting, and Individual Responsibilities

IV. The Family Mission, Keeping the Faith, Relating to Relatives and Friends, and Supporting Community

V. Raising Children: Partner Collaboration, Responsibilities, and Discipline

VI. Problem Solving, Decision Making, and Forgiveness

Note that the outline above may be different than what you decide on. First, talk this out. Second, refer to notes you have created as you went through this book. Make notes about what is important to you.

WEEK X:
COUPLE'S COMMUNICATION ABOUT SEX

Focus Question: How do we learn what we need and want from each other sexually?

Discussion: Most couples have figured out what pleases them at a basic level. As we start this discussion, we are in effect in the middle of the conversation the two of you are having or have had. You already know a lot.

However, many younger couples, perhaps you, do not know enough about relationships and sex to sustain intimacy for longer periods of time. Here is what many don't know. They don't know completely what they need and want. Even though many of you who are engaged or just married have found satisfaction in your sexual practice, for most couples there is a lot more to learn.

Life appears to trick young lovers. Some of you may be aware of this. Life limits the duration of romance, and after a seemingly all-too-short period of time, the charged romantic energy the two of you so enjoyed is no longer there. Then you will need to deal with larger questions, among them what it means to have continued friendship and have trust, fun, play, intimacy, and frequent sex. It is not necessarily inventing sex between the two of you all

After the Wedding Cake A11

over again. It is that this new phase of your relationship may require a smarter and more intentional sexuality.

What happens too often in early relationships is that your mutual admiration shifts to competition and then, of course, conflict. In fact it is sometimes considered a stage marriages must go through. Competition and conflict are the default setting in our culture. You may think this does not apply to you but you and your mate have been bombarded with ideas of competition all of your lives. To have a successful sexual relationship, the two of you will need to maintain the basis of compatibility. To have a good marriage at all and, of course, great sex, most of you will need to consciously move your marriage away from competition into a state of cooperation.

Even though you may have had pretty good sex already, the understanding of differences in how each of you reaches an orgasm is important. This may for many of you take some learning and trial and error. Also the longer you have a relationship, the more things like outside demands of work and, if you have children, of raising children are actually exhausting. And more than that, the many factors of stress can steal the joy of sex and fun in your relationship.

Assignment: If you have not had the discussions about sexuality and intimacy recommended in the sections about creating your personal, private covenant, please do so. Please read the chapter of this book on sex. By no means is what is written here about sexuality the final word. What is said in a few pages is meant to put you on a better track with your sex life.

This is the time to have a reflective conversation about your sex life. Reaffirm what you know, what you need and want, and how and when you agree to talk about it. What you know and decide will not be perfect, but if you are not comfortable discussing your sex life, it is possible to put it off for far too long.

Sex education is one big key to a successful marriage. Finding a good book discussing all of the aspects of sex is a good move. Please follow through. Even if you think you know a lot or actually may know a lot, having a sexual guide that you can talk about together and also read over a period of time is a preferred and good support to your relationship.

If you belong to a major religious denomination, then do check out what sexual guides are available in your faith tradition. Surprisingly, some religious organizations have good books with basic information. Also, you may find helpful resources at the end of this book. Of course feel free to do your own Internet search.

WEEK XI:
COUPLE'S COMMUNICATION ABOUT MONEY

Focus Question: What are our money values?

Discussion: There are many money factors that can sabotage a marriage relationship. They include not having mutual goals, making bad choices about credit, buying items you can't afford that can wait for another time, having no savings plan, and not being savvy about the good ways to use your credit union or bank.

The biggest issue, after the obvious one of being employed and having an income flow, is the question of values. I mean your personal values have more to do with whether your family is financially successful or not. Whether you start your life out as a poor couple or you come from money, your values will either contribute to your harmony or to your discord. Harmony and mutuality in money decisions, contribute to success.

Many of you will have had rudimentary discussions about what you believe, what you want, and how you spend money. However, this is a continuing conversation because individual values also reflect the complexity of a person. Some of you may take this discussion lightly but not taking it seriously is often at the root of marriage discord and poverty. Also, it is amazing how needing to be right about money decisions and how the nastiness of competition can rear its ugly head. However, the longer you are together, the greater your opportunity to learn, and the more you will, perhaps, know how to handle whatever money you have.

Assignment: Talk out how you will sustain yourselves, what jobs and money are available to you, where you will work, where you will live, what your money objectives are, and where you see yourselves together in five years. Now is also the time to discuss your goals to make sure that they don't conflict and are relatively compatible.

However, the most important conversation is about your values and approach to money. Many arguments result from a conflict of where money should be spent. Discuss what you learned from your parents and others about spending and budgeting. Please do not simply attempt to make this an easy conversation. This is a good time to talk out preferences and what you want money to do for you.

As an experiment, make a budget. How do you get along doing this? Do you have any ideas about who will keep and balance the checking account? Will you set an individual spending limit above which you will not go without consulting your partner? There is no one right way to run a marriage or a family. The question here is what will your way be?

WEEK XII:
COUPLE'S COMMUNICATION ABOUT IN-LAWS AND FAMILY

Focus Question: What truths about your families do you need to know and share?

Discussion: You no doubt have had a lot of conversation about families and background. This is a necessary discussion but one that could lead to touchy points. If all of your family members, those close and distant, like the two of you for the kind of people you are and as a couple, count yourself as very fortunate. There many, many family groupings that are healthy and stable, but not all.

Family conflict is more common than many admit. Unfortunately, there are often members of your family who will not like or appreciate you as a couple. There may be some who even will try to sabotage your marriage. Families often have members with dominant and destructive personalities or those who want to control your lives. There are some who want to turn you and your partner against each other. There are parents who do not believe that the daughter-in-law or the son-in-law is good enough for their child. There can also be family members that pose serious dangers. The worst scenarios can come up with family members who are addicted or are batterers, or who are abusers or have serious untreated mental illnesses.

Assignment: If you have not had an extensive discussion about your parents and your extended families, now is the time. This is also the time to discuss how you will resolve problems and ensure communication with each other. If you have never before written out what you know and hope for with communicating together, even if this is a short paragraph, now is the time to do it. Family conflicts can also turn into huge communication challenges.

Appendix II

A Communication Guide for Couples

What you know and how you communicate what you know is a critical part of marriage. In this section I will give you a summary of critical communication skills and ideas. I also lay out in detail a universal model or framework for both communication and listening.

A communication is a message given and a message received. A mere message, words in any form, is a message. A communication takes place when your partner receives and hears that message. Some of you may already practice reflective listening in which you can acknowledge and express the message which is given. That is a great practice.

First, here are my ten important relationship communication tips. These are of fundamental importance:

1. It is very helpful for a couple to create a physically and mentally safe place, a so-called safe vessel, for communication.

2. There is a lot of advice couples receive about hedging on the truth so as to not hurt your partner's feelings. However, in this book you are encouraged to practice speaking truth to the best of your ability from the very beginning. It is necessary for each to decide to speak your truth-not at all an easy task-and to move away from wanting to be appreciated for one's "act." It is not much of a relationship if your partner likes you for your act and not for the real you.

3. Along with speaking one's truth comes the need to honor the other by listening and especially by not adding judgment and criticism to what will inevitably be vulnerability that comes from being truthful.

4. A huge communication necessity is learning to authentically give and receive compliments and gratitude-daily.

5. The role of the critic needs to be eliminated from your communication style. All of us are exposed to criticism and too often all of us are critical.

Instead each of you is encouraged to actually listen and then speak honestly, having really heard what your partner has said.

6. You are encouraged to learn what projection is and in general how to eliminate it. Projection occurs in part by assuming what is true for you has to be true for your partner. Projection can lead to judging and too often the ideas of projections are wrong.

7. Learning and practicing the use of "I-statements" is a helpful communication form and skill. The famous family therapist Murray Bowen popularized it. It is a useful practice in daily conversation even when there is no argument or tense issue.

8. Improving critical thinking improves couples communication. The practice of the ORID (Objective, Reflective, Interpretive, Decisional) form of communication can help couples more quickly understand one another even when issues are complex. The discussion below gives a detailed explanation. This approach usually improves listening and helps create common ground.

9. If a marriage is thought of as successful, it usually means couples are unified in basic thinking and goals. Couples need to make an absolute decision that they will cease attempting to win or be right as opposed to working together on their relationship. Always insisting on being right leads too often to disputes and arguing and win-lose and lose-lose outcomes. If you as a couple do not make this basic decision, all communication methods will ultimately fail to bring about intimacy. This means eliminating the win-lose struggles, stopping competition, and deciding that co-operation is the dominant practice for the two of you.

10. This one is big. Each partner must understand that to bring about positive change, one changes one's own self and not the partner! Not having this kind of understanding can lead to many of the following communication problems: discussed below..

The inability to forgive.can show up as a major communication issue. The very statement, made in a timely manner-for example, "I'm sorry"-can go a long way to making repairs necessary to restore healthy communication. You need to be prepared to own your mistake(s) and possibly explain what you have learned from it (them).

So in thinking about communication hurdles-for example, the need for reflections and possibly forgiveness-one problematic situation stands out.

A major communication mistake is blurting out an accusation, a so-called absolute or flat statement, that may be fueled by suspicion, impulse, or anger. Hopefully you may learn the tactic of delaying any speech in order to buy time that will allow you to compose your own thoughts. It may be more helpful to ask your thoughts as a question rather than stating them as a judgmental absolute statement. This does not mean forming a question as a "gotcha." It means, instead, asking a genuine question and seeking actual information.

The Power of Creating a Context: The Bigger Picture

What the above communication ideas and tips are about and indeed what this whole book is about is ways of telling the success story of your wonderful relationship. This telling of your story means you are creating a context for your marriage. Every time anyone tells a story that is important to someone else, it is called creating a context.

Let's take this idea of context a step further. Every successful communication and every beneficial action depends on each of us knowing or having a good context, a collection of facts, ideas, or story, that informs us. The act of telling a story or sharing important ideas is called contexting. What makes a couple's communications work well are all the shared ideas-that is, contexts-between the two of you. I like the statement, "What breath is to the body, contexting is to the mind."

An Advanced Lesson in Communication

Many years ago I joined my colleagues in popularizing a set of ideas or an approach that effectively promotes communication and can create helpful contexts. Today, the shorthand name for this approach is called by the acronym O.R.I.D., which is popularly used by ToP (Technology of Participation) facilitators and the Institute of Cultural Affairs. This method is very sophisticated and yet is simple to learn. What it can do for you as a couple is create an even more effective way of sharing your ideas with each other, hugely increase your critical thinking skills, and give you a model that allows both of you to become in-depth listeners.

The model has four levels that are simple to learn but truly the model needs your mental daring, intellectual curiosity akin to an adventure, to make this method the most powerful and versatile communication tool you'll find anywhere. The names of the levels are: 1. Objective, 2. Reflective, 3. Interpretive, and 4. Decisional. If you regularly practice the ideas that go with these four levels, you will find yourself becoming a more powerful communicator and listener. When both partners use this method, you may well find that there is a larger common ground between you, your common memory usually becomes broader, and often the quality of your mutual decisions becomes better.

An example of this method for those who want to see a step-by-step approach is offered below. This is an established personal and business method used all over the world. When we first used this approach, it was called the Art Form Method and was used to create a conversation format for artworks, readings, and movies. You will also find some explanations of this method on the Internet. Following are sample questions from this kind of conversation. For the sake of example, we are using a painting as a mutual object of interest.

Objective Level questions seek basic facts.

1. In this painting what objects do you see?

2. What colors do you see?

3. What people?

4. What animals?

Reflective Level questions relate emotions and recall; they are the kind that may grab you in the "gut" so to speak, and build on the objective level.

5. Where do you see expressions of emotions in this painting?

6. What emotions have you noticed this painting is bringing out in you?

7. What do like about this painting?

8. Do you remember seeing this painting or one like it anywhere else?

Interpretive Level questions ask about meaning, values, purpose, analysis, and so on.

9. In your opinion what statement is this artist making?

10. What are the people in this painting doing?

11. Are there levels of story revealed in this painting? What are they?

12. What significance could this painting have to someone? To you?

Decisional Level questions take in the first three levels and ask about what you would do or say about what you have learned.

13. The artist gave this painting a name but what name would you give the painting?

14. Who do you know that would benefit by seeing and experiencing this painting?

15. Where in your house would you hang this painting?

16. What friends would you share this painting with?

Now that you see how these questions work, you can use similar questions with any topic and any category. My friends Dennis Jennings and Judy Weddle, world-class facilitators, explain the levels as follows: The objective level of fact questions might be symbolized by the word "What?" The reflective questions to take in both feelings and memory can be symbolized by the word "Gut." The interpretive questions, "So what?" Finally, the decisional, "Now what?"

Here is one more story to help illustrate the four levels. Once I worked with a truly delightful woman who also had a mental illness called paranoid schizophrenia. She experienced both confusing unfocused days and some very bright good ones. To give her hope and as much as possible to encourage her continued learning, I taught her O.R.I.D.

Then I asked her what people would "stand for" the levels she had learned. She had recently seen the movie *Dragnet* and right away stated that the objective level was about detectives. "Give me the facts, just the facts, please." For the reflective level she chose actress Glen Close because she portrays scenes of "emotion and memory so well." For the interpretive level her choice was obvious for her. She chose world-famous Albert Einstein. And for the decisional, she chose John Kennedy. Why? "Because he was a man of action."

What you need to know is that you can use these four levels with any topic any time. What you need to do to truly make this method work in astounding and amazing ways is to practice it daily. It is unbelievable how well this approach works for shy people during a party or reception. You can use it with the news, with finding about each other's day, going to the grocery store, and every topic conceivable in the universe. Very importantly, it is a great LISTENING model.

It may be used sometimes in question form, in couple's conversations, in teamwork, in the development of a story, in the creation of a talk, in sales presentations, and in planning, only to name a few arenas. A wonderful book called *The Art of the Focused Conversation* available online and through bookstores, models 100 different ways to use O.R.I.D. in business and other organizations. There is a similar book for schools. It just happens to be a wonderful personal and family communication approach.

This method is used today by businesses, schools, government agencies, and what you would think of as average people on at least every continent and probably in almost every nation in the world. However, there appear to be people who have difficulty with the whole approach. Because this is a kind of discipline, there are some who find this method uncomfortable. It is mystifying that some people just can't use O.R.I.D. So while this method works for most people, it may not work for some.

Appendix III

The Covenant of Service and Mission

Many people find it difficult at first-not later on, but in the beginning-to think about relationships that include a personal and a family mission of service. This is also a collaboration for you as a couple and a broader covenant than most people consider when they think about marriage. So this appendix is written to offer extra help for those people who may be new to this idea.

In Part Three of this book we introduced the four covenants of marriage. In Appendix One it is included in the 12-week workshop for a successful marriage. The covenant everyone knows about has to do with the public vows that couples take in the marriage ceremony. The other covenants are more personal. The sexual or personal covenant is where you decide how you will talk about and practice all of the aspects of your personal relationship and of sexual intimacy. The Family Constitution is a covenant that creates the family ordering and organization. Most people can figure this out and write one for their family.

The last covenant is the Family Covenant of Service. Many families pride themselves in giving back, the act of reflecting gratitude and returning kindness, to their communities, country, and to people in the world. For them it is a natural expression of their connection to people and their faith. However, for many others the notion of service, unless it is somehow tied to something older or more traditional like the armed forces, is not familiar. Or perhaps they wrongly think this idea is for someone else and not for them.

In earlier parts of the book we have discussed some of the ways the world interacts with the couple. Now as a couple living in the new reality that shows up as multiple dimensions of community in our time, a couple's challenge is to take responsibility for experiencing it and creating it. What we have learned is that if we want clean air and water, relative peace, and a healthier existence, we all have a role to play. Community becomes hugely important for those of you who will be parents.

The covenant of service can be expressed in two parts. One part is individual, personal, and must be answered first by both partners. The focus question for this individual part of the covenant goes something like this, "What is my life calling?" or "What is it I must stand for and do to make my life worth living?" Notice that this question cannot be answered without the surroundings you find yourself in or your conscious or even unconscious idea of community.

Other secondary thoughts along with the one above are often about personal questions like: What it is that you find joy in? What activities bring you satisfaction and bliss? However, do not miss this question: "What really important thing is going on the world right now that if I miss being a part of it, my life will be diminished?" Now all of these questions when answered have a big impact on your relationship. While your partner cannot do your work, it is essential that these are shared and understood between the two of you.

The answers to these kinds of questions often start with your own intuition. You can also employ memory of places, people, and activities with which you are really connected. You can think of jobs or studies that excited you. All of these are probably intuitional flags that can guide you to your own mission statement. After this thought process, you may even be able to scribble out notions of your mission.

The process described above lets you look at yourself and your external world. It is also helpful to reflect inwardly about all of the notions and ideas that are suggested here. Here is another approach that takes inward reflection a step further. Take some time to think about the various events of your life that pop into your mind. What moments stand out as your best? What notions do they offer about your directions and your mission?

Take another trip through memory and recall your own inner child. What was it that made the little you happy? What caused sadness? Where did you as the kid need help or protection? These questions are relevant and can inform you about your wishes and passion.

At this point, with a leap of faith, look five years into the future and see how and what you would like to be. Write that down. Now look inside yourself again and ask how the little one, you as your inner child, would respond to that vision. If your notion is that you as the little one also like your 5-year vision, then you probably have a good one.

For some people the following gender-oriented approach may be easier. You might say something like, "As a woman among women, I am an advocate for child health and prenatal care." Or you could start by saying as a man among men and then continue with a statement about what is unique about you.

Then ask yourself if this statement fits with who you would be in five years. If so, think about the roles you might play. At this point you must add action words to your idea. It could sound like, "My mission is to assure the elements of medical care and education for children by speaking my truth and acting on their behalf so that kids everywhere are assured a bright future."

There is one final set of questions to check before completing your mission statement: How does the mission you have come up with fit your dominant interests and abilities? How passionate are you about the mission you have conceived? What is it you are doing now that might fit into your mission?

Well, you see, you probably have the real guts of a mission statement here. You may rethink and rewrite it later. Your challenge now may be to have the most mature and thoughtful conversations you have ever had with your partner. Not only can you and, no doubt, will you help one another with your ideas, you will need to sit down and hear each other's statements.

Are these missional ideas ones I can understand? Are they ideas which I really like, affirm, and with which I agree? As you compare your missional statements ask the following: "Is the direction of both statements compatible?" and "Is there anything in the basic missional ideas that would be so disruptive to us as a couple or family that it just would not work?" For example, if your future spouse is called to climb mountains nine months of the year and you are creating a child development center, is this the relationship for you? Maybe yes? Maybe no? It is very good to get clarity on each statement. From there it is much easier to write a family mission statement.

Thoughts on Family Mission

Talk out what it is that you both believe in. Where is there common ground? What is it the two of you believe in or stand for? What light turned on as you talked out your thoughts, passions, hopes, and directions? Write down, from what you know now, what might be your family mission.

Whatever you write is unique in some way to you. There is no right or wrong to this. You can always clarify and make changes later. When you've finished with this intellectual part of the exercise, ask yourselves out loud how you feel.

Our Family Mission

To express care and love for each other …
To consciously be one another's partner …
To create a loving home in which children can prosper …
To do economically and emotionally satisfying work …
To bless others as we have been blessed …
To worship together …
And to serve others that they may know their blessings.

A longer family mission could have statements about your commitments to each other, to the creation of your home and your life together. It could include your commitment to finding and creating communities in which the health and well-being of all people is promoted. It could talk about how you see faith and work coming together to make a vocation.

You have been given ideas about how to compose a mission statement for each of you and also ideas about the family mission. It is up to you to take the leap of faith to make these two mission statements happen for you.

Appendix IV

Example of a Private or Personal Covenant

You may have already written your private covenant after you explored your public covenant, and actually did the reflection exercise on what is important to you. For those of you who might need it, here is one version of the private covenant. Note that every covenant has to begin somewhere, even if it is brief.

From Joe and Mary Ann:
I embrace you as my one and only partner in intimacy, and I believe in our time together we will both touch the divine.

Because of what we have learned from parents and friends, we commit to monogamy.

The first principle in our private life as well as our sex life is communication. We continually pledge to make it safe for one another to tell it the way it is. We intend to learn from each other and teach each other as we grow together.

The second principle we commit to is making anger and conflict resolution as the biggest priority for both of us. We intend to share our lives in love and cooperation.

The third principle we commit to is reserving time and giving each other our presence. This includes time for dates, loving and hugging, and sex. This means making you, my partner and soul mate, a priority in my life.

We understand that our loving and intimacy is about learning together so that we may care for each other's emotional needs.

We celebrate our sex not just to satiate our drives but as a conscious pathway to intimacy, a greater sense of spiritual unity.

We commit to being all in. Our goal is to cherish every kiss, every hug, and every touch. And we commit to do these actions, to the best of our ability, all the time. We intend to have nutty, happy fun, and, so to speak, to swing from the chandeliers. Our mutual question is "How do I continue to cherish you?"

22877156R00143

Made in the USA
Columbia, SC
03 August 2018